D0174748

Wolf Songs

THE CLASSIC COLLECTION OF WRITING ABOUT WOLVES
EDITED *by* ROBERT BUSCH

SIERRA CLUB BOOKS
San Francisco

THE SIERRA CLUB, founded in 1892 by John Muir, has devoted itself to the study and protection of the earth's scenic and ecological resources—mountains, wetlands, woodlands, wild shores and rivers, deserts and plains. The publishing program of the Sierra Club offers books to the public as a nonprofit educational service in the hope that they may enlarge the public's understanding of the Club's basic concerns. The point of view expressed in each book, however, does not necessarily represent that of the Club. The Sierra Club has some sixty chapters coast to coast, in Canada, Hawaii, and Alaska. For information about how you may participate in its programs to preserve wilderness and the quality of life, please address inquiries to Sierra Club, 730 Polk Street, San Francisco, CA 94109.

To Sunny,
WHO DESERVED SO MUCH MORE

CONTENTS

ACKNOWLEDGMENTS

THANKS ARE DUE to the many organizations that patiently answered my questions during the research for this book: the Canadian Wildlife Service, U.S. Fish & Wildlife Service (especially Steven H. Fritts, Northern Rocky Mountain Wolf Coordinator), World Wildlife Fund (Canada), Alberta Fish & Game Division, British Columbia Ministry of the Environment, Alaska Wildlife Alliance, and Wolf Haven.

To Jim Cohee, my thanks for his faith in this project. And thanks to the wild wolves of the Cariboo for the inspiration for this book—may you live long and run free.

Maybe
in time
Beast and Bird shall
take back their earth
   of which they
   kindly invited
   mankind
to live:
In trust
that
   all would be well.

MARGUERITE H. REID

CHAPTER ONE

Introduction: The Past of the Wolf

ROBERT H. BUSCH

ROBERT H. BUSCH *was born in Calgary,
Alberta, and graduated from the University of Calgary,
where he received the APEGGA Gold Medal and
The Queen's Prize. His articles on natural history
have appeared in numerous national magazines,
including* Nature Canada, Country Journal, *and*
Wildlife Conservation. *He is an active member of a
number of animal conservation organizations, and has a
particular interest in predators. He lives in the Cariboo
Mountains of central British Columbia, where he is
sometimes lulled to sleep by wild wolf songs.*

I HEARD MY FIRST wolf song on an icy December evening. From a snow-frosted beach by a mountain lake
came a wavering chorus of howls that formed an eerie
wilderness symphony. And to many people the wolf *is*
the very symbol of wilderness, the symbol of freedom,
and a reminder that there is Something Out There
stronger than ourselves.

But in the past, the wolf suffered from people mistakenly attributing to it such ignoble traits as viciousness, bloodthirsty hunger, and insatiable lusts. Much
of this reputation originated in Europe, where it became entrenched in legend and in fable.

Fables using the imagery of the wolf can be traced
back to ancient times. The stories attributed to Aesop
(c. 600 B.C.) emphasized cunning, deceit, and vicious-

ness as attributes of the wolf. The story of "The Boy Who Cried Wolf" and later tales, such as "The Three Little Pigs," have for centuries ingrained in children's minds a negative caricature of the wolf as an evil creature, to be feared and hated.

In the Bible (John 10:12), Jesus describes himself as a shepherd protecting the sheep from the wolf. And Lord Byron wrote of an attacker "coming down like a wolf on the fold."

More often than any other animal, it was the wolf that was endowed with supernatural powers in the tales of old Europe. In the Middle Ages, fantastic werewolf sagas resulted in the slaughter of thousands of innocent animals and hundreds of falsely labeled humans. Unfortunate children with physical or mental deficiencies were often thought to be reincarnations of werewolves or to be orphans actually raised by wolves. Many were put to death for their imaginary sins.

The wolf's poor reputation resulted in predictably poor treatment at the hands of humans. As we evolved from hunters to farmers, we ruthlessly eliminated all potential competition for land and livestock. King Edgar the Peaceful in tenth-century England even allowed his loyal citizens to pay their taxes in wolf heads. The war waged on wolves led to their early extermination from the British Isles: the last wolf in Scotland was killed in 1743, and Ireland's wolf population was eliminated by 1776.

The fairytale now called "Little Red Riding Hood," originally written in the late 1600s, emphasized the ravenous hunger of the wolf, laced with heavy sexual overtones. Even today we describe a lusting human male as a "real wolf."

T. H. White's *The Book of Beasts*, a translation of twelfth-century Latin accounts, describes the wolf as "a rapacious beast . . . hankering for gore." Shakespeare characterized appetite as the "universal wolf." And today's expressions of people "keeping the wolf from the door" or being "hungry as a wolf" continue to perpetuate the notion that wolves are characterized by voracious hunger.

In the minds of many Europeans, the wolf was a vicious predator that lurked behind every tree, waiting to attack and devour the unwary. Legends of man-eating wolves are numerous, especially in France and in Russia. Weaving through many a Russian folktale is the fanciful sight of Russian sleighs dashing through the dark Siberian woods, pursued by packs of slavering wolves.

But underlying much of the negative imagery associated with the wolf was a thread of respect. For instance, some Saxon kings named themselves after wolves in hopes of gaining the cunning and strength of wolves. And in the New World, the wolf attained almost religious status.

In North America the wolf was well respected by the native Indians and Eskimos. Many tribes revered the wolf for its hunting abilities, intelligence, and position as the provider of food to its pack. As such, the wolf became a "totem," or god figure, to many of these tribes.

Northwest coastal Indians divided their people into two clans, both named after intelligent animals: the wolf and the raven. Cheyenne Indians rubbed wolf fur on their arrows to give them improved hunting skills. And many tribes had wolf warrior societies in which the warriors draped themselves in wolf skins or dangled wolf paws from their belts, in hope that the hunting skills of the wolf would rub off.

To some tribes, the wolf was a messenger from the spirit world, an accolade bestowed on few other creatures. The Pawnee and Oto Indians made wolf bundles, packets of sacred items wrapped in wolf skins used in sacred ceremonies to appease the gods.

■

Unfortunately, when Europeans emigrated to North America they brought with them their legends and beliefs. The North American wolf was to pay a terrible price as a result. The taming of the American wilderness resulted in the slaughter of many of its wild inhabitants, and perhaps no animal suffered more than the wolf. It is ironic that the term "howling wilderness," a concept venerated by modern conservationists, derived from the animal that the settlers hated most, the wolf.

A staple food of the prairie wolf was the buffalo. In fact, Lewis and Clark referred to the wolf as the "shepherd of the buffalo." But as settlers invaded the prairie, the buffalo was considered competition to the herds of domestic animals that had been brought out west. Furthermore, white settlers knew that by killing off the buffalo they could jeopardize the very survival of the despised Indians, who depended so heavily on it. As a result, millions of buffalo were slaughtered and their huge carcasses added the reek of death to the fresh sage smell that once wafted across the virgin prairie.

The millions of slaughtered buffalo that littered the plains attracted thousands of predators and caused a temporary jump in predator numbers. But the increase did not last. With the buffalo nearly exterminated, the wolf turned to the domestic stock that was now grazing in its place. Cattle, sheep, and chickens became easy prey for the wily wolf.

Farmers and ranchers fought back with an intensity completely out of proportion to their actual losses. The natural desire to protect livestock was compounded by their unnatural fear of the wolf. The irrational fear led to unbelievable cruelty.

Wolves were shot, strangled, set afire, dynamited, bludgeoned, and stabbed. Leg-hold traps were used to capture wolves, which were then set free after their jaws were wired shut. Wolves were infected with mange and then released to spread this deadly disease among their wild cousins. Tons of strychnine were set out across the prairie, resulting in the deaths of hundreds of thousands of wolves, coyotes, birds, and rodents. Hunters cornered wolves and then set their dogs on them, ironically pitting modern canids against their distant cousins.

The wolf also suffered because of its eating habits. Because it is an eater of carrion as well as fresh meat, the wolf was falsely blamed for thousands of natural livestock deaths. As a scapegoat, the ubiquitous wolf made an easy target.

Many jurisdictions established wolf bounties, which

became legal justification for wholesale slaughter on an unprecedented scale. Bounties on wolves became an important source of income for hundreds of eager hunters, many of whom would have gladly performed the service for free. The carnage was relentless. Some wolf hunters of the late 1800s claimed lifetime totals of tens of thousands of wolves.

The few remaining wolves became legendary outlaws, demigods with names such as Old Three Toes, the Phantom, and the King of Currumpaw. The bounty hunters who finally slaughtered these individuals became heroes: the killer of Old Three Toes was presented with a gold watch.

In the mid-1850s, the steel leg-hold trap invented by Sewell Newhouse became widely available. The inventor wrote that his trap "going before the axe and the plow, forms the prow with which iron-clad civilization is pushing back barbaric solitude, causing the bear and the beaver to give place to the wheatfield, the library and the piano." It also caused the tortured suffering of thousands of wolves.

Recreational hunting placed additional threats on wolf populations. As technology advanced, the natural survival skills of the wolf were pushed to their limits. Hunters chased the animal on foot, on horseback, and much later in trucks, by plane, and by snowmobile.

Theodore Roosevelt, the so-called conservationist president, once attended a wolf hunt accompanied by an entourage of 137 dogs, 60 horses, and 44 humans. Hopelessly outnumbered by such gun-crazy mobs, wolves died by the thousands.

As the devastating march of "progress" pushed back the wilderness, the wolf went with it. By the 1930s, the wolf had been virtually eliminated from the western plains of the United States. It has never returned. By the 1940s, the last stronghold for the prairie wolf was in Canada, but there too wolf control measures took a horrible toll.

Even national parks and preserves were no refuge for the wolf. In misguided attempts to save herds of park elk or deer, park rangers killed hundreds of park wolves. The largest wolf on record in the United States was killed in Alaska in 1939 by a government hunter. In Canada, the largest wolf ever taken was shot in Jasper National Park in 1945, killed by a park warden whose sworn duty was "to protect the park."

The popular opinion of the day is further exemplified by a 1955 article in *Field & Stream* magazine that glorified the aerial shooting of wolves. The article was entitled "Strafing Arctic Killers." Its author was future Alaska governor Jay Hammond.

■

Finally, in the 1960s, in the wake of a rising interest in the very viability of the planet, a more accepting attitude toward wild animals began to appear. In 1961, scientists concerned with the many perils facing animals the world over founded the World Wildlife Fund. A year later, Rachel Carson's classic *Silent Spring* awakened many to the potential fate of planet Earth. In 1969, both Greenpeace and the Friends of the Earth were founded, two of the many environmental groups that became powerful lobbying forces. In 1970, the first Earth Day was held. And in 1973, the International Convention on the Trade in Endangered Species (CITES) was established.

By the 1970s, the "greening" of the world resulted in a maturing of attitudes toward its wild inhabitants. In 1972, recreational shooting of wolves from airplanes in Alaska was finally abolished. One of the last wolf bounties in Canada, in the province of Ontario, was dropped the same year.

In 1973, the wolf received legal protection as an endangered species in the contiguous forty-eight states, except for Minnesota, where it was classified as threatened. The role of the predator in the wild had finally become recognized, and an enlightened public became more accepting of the wolf and of other large predators.

No one knows how many wolves were slaughtered before their public image finally began to change. No one counted. No one cared. But it has been estimated that over a million wolves lost their lives and that at least another million individuals of other species died through indiscriminate trapping and poisoning programs.

This book is presented in their memory.

CHAPTER TWO

Thinking Like a Mountain

ALDO LEOPOLD

*ALDO LEOPOLD was born in 1887 in Iowa.
He joined the U.S. Forest Service in 1909, and helped
form America's first wilderness area in 1924. He is widely
recognized as one of the first of the great conservationists,
and one of the first to call for the preservation of wild
places. In 1933, he chaired the game management
department at the University of Wisconsin, and later
became an adviser on conservation to the United Nations.
He died in 1948 while fighting a grass fire on a
neighbor's farm. His classic A Sand County Almanac
was published in 1949, after his death. Leopold was
posthumously named to the National Wildlife Federation's
Conservation Hall of Fame in 1965 and was honored by a
John Burroughs Medal for his life work. The Aldo
Leopold Wilderness Area, in the Black Range of
New Mexico, was named in his honor. As the Wisconsin
State Journal (September 19, 1965, p. 4) noted,
"Aldo Leopold died in 1948, but he stands tall
today, like a giant pine tree, visible from
the . . . concrete racetracks of civilization."*

A DEEP CHESTY BAWL echoes from rimrock to rimrock, rolls down the mountain, and fades into the far
blackness of the night. It is an outburst of wild defiant
sorrow, and of contempt for all the adversities of the
world.

Every living thing (and perhaps many a dead one as
well) pays heed to that call. To the deer it is a reminder
of the way of all flesh, to the pine a forecast of midnight

9

scuffles and of blood upon the snow, to the coyote a promise of gleanings to come, to the cowman a threat of red ink at the bank, to the hunter a challenge of fang against bullet. Yet behind these obvious and immediate hopes and fears there lies a deeper meaning, known only to the mountain itself. Only the mountain has lived long enough to listen objectively to the howl of a wolf.

Those unable to decipher the hidden meaning know nevertheless that it is there, for it is felt in all wolf country, and distinguishes that country from all other land. It tingles in the spine of all who hear wolves by night, or who scan their tracks by day. Even without sight or sound of wolf, it is implicit in a hundred small events: the midnight whinny of a pack horse, the rattle of rolling rocks, the bound of a fleeing deer, the way shadows lie under the spruces. Only the ineducable tyro can fail to sense the presence or absence of wolves, or the fact that mountains have a secret opinion about them.

My own conviction on this score dates from the day I saw a wolf die. We were eating lunch on a high rimrock, at the foot of which a turbulent river elbowed its way. We saw what we thought was a doe fording the torrent, her breast awash in white water. When she climbed the bank toward us and shook out her tail, we realized our error: it was a wolf. A half-dozen others, evidently grown pups, sprang from the willows and all joined in a welcoming mêlée of wagging tails and playful maulings. What was literally a pile of wolves writhed and tumbled in the center of an open flat at the foot of our rimrock.

In those days we had never heard of passing up a chance to kill a wolf. In a second we were pumping lead into the pack, but with more excitement than accuracy: how to aim a steep downhill shot is always confusing. When our rifles were empty, the old wolf was down, and a pup was dragging a leg into impassable slide-rocks.

We reached the old wolf in time to watch a fierce green fire dying in her eyes. I realized then, and have known ever since, that there was something new to me in those eyes—something known only to her and to the mountain. I was young then, and full of trigger-itch; I thought that because fewer wolves meant more deer, that no wolves would mean hunters' paradise. But after seeing the green fire die, I sensed that neither the wolf nor the mountain agreed with such a view.

■

Since then I have lived to see state after state extirpate its wolves. I have watched the face of many a newly wolf-less mountain, and seen the south-facing slopes wrinkle with a maze of new deer trails. I have seen every edible bush and seedling browsed, first to anaemic desuetude, and then to death. I have seen every edible tree defoliated to the height of a saddlehorn. Such a mountain looks as if someone had given God a new pruning shears, and forbidden Him all other exercise. In the end the starved bones of the hoped-for deer herd, dead of its own too-much, bleach with the bones of the dead sage, or molder under the high-lined junipers.

I now suspect that just as a deer herd lives in mortal fear of its wolves, so does a mountain live in mortal fear of its deer. And perhaps with better cause, for while a buck pulled down by wolves can be replaced in two or three years, a range pulled down by too many deer may fail of replacement in as many decades.

So also with cows. The cowman who cleans his range of wolves does not realize that he is taking over the wolf's job of trimming the herd to fit the range. He has not learned to think like a mountain. Hence we have dustbowls, and rivers washing the future into the sea.

■

We all strive for safety, prosperity, comfort, long life, and dullness. The deer strives with his supple legs, the cowman with trap and poison, the statesman with pen, the most of us with machines, votes, and dollars, but it all comes to the same thing: peace in our time. A measure of success in this is all well enough, and perhaps is a requisite to objective thinking, but too much safety seems to yield only danger in the long run. Perhaps this is behind Thoreau's dictum: In wildness is the salvation of the world. Perhaps this is the hidden meaning in the howl of the wolf, long known among mountains, but seldom perceived among men.

CHAPTER THREE

Growing Up Wild

R. D. LAWRENCE

R. D. LAWRENCE *was born at sea near Vigo, Spain, in 1921. He was raised in Spain and England before emigrating to Canada in 1954, where he rapidly became one of Canada's best-known naturalists. His books include* Cry Wild *(1970),* The North Runner *(1979),* The Zoo That Never Was *(1981),* The Ghost Walker *(1983), and many others. He lives in central Ontario with his wife Sharon and his two wolves Tundra and Taiga.*

DURING ONE of our short walks together Wa's rashness got him into trouble with an old, somewhat irascible raccoon, who had reserved for himself an apartment inside the trunk of a big, downed maple. For three years One Ear had occupied these quarters during spring, summer, and fall at those times when his rambles did not take him too far away from its location.

He was a big fellow, battle-scarred, his right ear chewed off at some time, probably by another male during a fight over a female. He had turned up at our feeder one evening, there to sit like some hairy, miniature Buddha ingesting the goodies that were always set out for our forest friends morning and evening. The feeder in question, one of several strategically located around the farm house, was fastened to the kitchen windowsill; it consisted of a two-foot-by-three-foot tray connected to the ground by a leaning pole that acted as a walkway. During the day it contained seed and peanut bits for the birds and squirrels and, of course, for Scruffy and his ilk; after supper, table scraps and a fresh supply of seeds and nuts were put out for our many raccoon friends and for the flying squirrels, who always enjoyed a nice bit of protein when they could get it and who alternated between chewing left-over bones and stuffing themselves on seeds.

One Ear was a total stranger when he first showed up, but being aged and wise, he knew a good thing when he saw it. From that evening onward he appeared with regular punctuality soon after the feeder had been re-stocked. In no time, he allowed himself to be fed by hand, accepting tidbits such as marshmallows and sandwiches of peanut butter and honey with a sort of regal condescension.

One Ear was far from amused when a bumptious male wolf pup entered his recumbent log one morning and within this sanctum performed some unspeakable act almost under his pugilistic nose. My attention had wandered to Matta, who was attempting to crawl down a groundhog burrow, so I was not aware that Wa had trespassed until I heard One Ear's growl and Wa's scream of utter terror. I knew what had taken place before I completed the turn that would point me toward the raccoon's fortress.

Sure enough, I was in time to observe the appearance of one hysterical wolf cub whose legs were moving exceedingly fast but whose body seemed to emerge in slow motion; a few seconds later the reason for this anomaly became evident. Holding fast to Wa's ruler-straight tail was One Ear, who, despite his most strenuous efforts, was being pulled out of his redoubt by the screaming cub.

I was about to step across the two or three yards that separated me from the scene of the action when Matta did the unexpected. Emitting as deep a growl as she was capable of, she charged, taking the raccoon from the rear and delivering a series of fast snaps to his bulging bottom. Her teeth could not possibly penetrate One Ear's fur, but her attack caused him to let go of Wa's tail in order to turn swiftly, stare in unbelief at this second intruder, and then, hunching his shoulders, going into a fighting crouch and baring his not inconsiderable armament, he charged the little bitch. Meanwhile, Wa was high-tailing it for the rendezvous, yowling incessantly.

Little Matta, now that she had committed herself, stood her ground, but before any further skirmishes could take place, I reached the combatants. One Ear was booted unceremoniously in the rump, whereupon, essaying one vengeful snap at my right Kodiak boot, he dived back into his now somewhat odoriferous log. As she was rashly about to follow her fleeing enemy, I grabbed Matta by the scruff and lifted her to safety. We were only halfway back to the rendezvous when Tundra came leaping into the woods, tail curled, ears pricked forward, the glint of battle in his eye. Evidently Joan had heard Wa's laments—she couldn't very well help hearing them—and had let Tundra off his chain, following him as fast as she could go.

Inasmuch as Tundra did not stop to comfort Wa, as

one would have expected, I concluded that he had heard
One Ear's growls, and perhaps Matta's, and had not tar-
ried, for if there was one thing that Tundra wanted to
taste more than Scruffy, it was One Ear.

When all the parties came together and Wa, com-
forted in Joan's arms, became silent, I explained the situation to my wife as I checked the cub's tail. The
raccoon's teeth had torn the skin a little, but that was
all; it was nothing to worry about. However, as I was
examining him, I realized that either he had had a
bowel movement in the log and thus aroused One Ear's
ire on two counts or he had been unable to control himself and had fired a salvo while the raccoon's teeth were
clamped to his tail. In any event, he was in a rather
disgusting condition, and a goodly amount of the waste
that plastered his nether regions had transferred itself
to Joan's white blouse, a fact that she noticed only when
my gaze was directed toward her person and my nose
signaled that all was not well. Wa, terrified and screaming, had aroused all that was good and kind and ma-
ternal in Joan; Wa, almost unscathed and plastered in
manure, was able instantly to trigger a series of almost
opposite reactions in my wife. She did stoop so as not
to drop him from too high, but his return to the ground
was rapid and unceremonious. As Joan turned to run
home, already beginning to unbutton her blouse, she
called over her shoulder, "You *filthy* little pig!" But an
hour later all was forgiven, and Wa, thanks once again
to Tundra, was clean enough to receive a thorough
sponging with baby shampoo and warm water, an act

of kindness and cleanliness that our wolf objected to more than to the tail chomping he had received.

Matta, for the first time in her young life, was the heroine of the hour. The praise, endearments, and petting she received from Joan, in addition to the surreptitious pieces of my supper steak that she was fed, more than rewarded her for what I suspected was an instinctive act, a sort of premature self-defense reaction. But I did not utter such a base thought aloud.

A week later Wa walked himself and his sister into trouble of another kind. The result of this escapade created an even greater outcry from both cubs; but it ended with positive results.

On this occasion I led the cubs away from the evaporator house early one morning and then allowed them to select our route, doing so partly because I wanted them to exercise freedom of choice and partly out of curiosity, wishing to see what they would do and what direction they would take.

Initially each wolf was intent on pursuing its own affairs, Wa going one way, Matta another, but neither of them running too far head on their own. At the end of half an hour we were still within the edge of the northern part of the maple woods and only about a quarter of a mile from the house. But at this point Wa suddenly elected to follow a definite course, though his reasons for doing so were never to become apparent to me.

He was sniffing at the entrance to a chipmunk burrow, while Matta was pawing apart a cluster of fungi that grew on a rotting branch, when he stopped, lifted his head, and stared toward the east, ears pricked forward and tail held high. Looking in the same direction, I failed to detect anything out of the ordinary. Through the thinning maples the small, eastern clearing was visible; beyond it, the mixed forest that led to the East Ridge basked quietly in the new sun. I listened carefully, but only the sound of a soft breeze coursing through the treetops was audible to my ears.

Wa moved forward, stepping out almost daintily, lifting each leg high and placing his paws with care. Matta abandoned her task to stare at him, then she ran ahead of me and joined her brother, maintaining her usual walking pace and lagging just behind him. I followed.

It was clear that Wa was now intent on some definite errand. He continued moving eastward, his pace constant, his senses oblivious to those local inducements through which we were passing. Only Matta looked up when a blue jay launched itself out of a high branch, swooped low over the clearing, and flapped away into the trees on the other side. Wa kept his gaze fixed ahead, as though he were following a compass direction. The pace he was setting allowed me to keep up with both cubs by walking only a little faster than usual, the distance between us remaining a constant twenty to twenty-five strides. A short time later it became evident that Wa would take us directly to the ridge.

In due course we came within sight of one of my own trails where this converged with a game track only yards away from the spot where I usually ascended the rise. Wa increased his pace slightly; soon he was climbing the mossy slope, Matta close to his heels.

When we all gained the top, Wa led south instead of north, a direction along which I had never taken him. He still had about him that purposeful bearing so often displayed by a dog who leaves home intent on going directly from A to B and stopping not to wet or sniff. But the reason for such deliberate travel was not at all evident. I knew that if we continued to follow the ridge southward for another quarter of a mile, we would arrive at an old, largely overgrown homestead clearing in the center of which lay the remains of a log cabin built there, according to local history, by the first owner of the farm, who had come here from England in 1861. All that was left of the building were a few rotting pieces of hand-squared log and some pathetic, broken relics discarded by the former occupants: bits of china, rusty pieces of an old woodstove, and so on, showing here and there among the grasses and stone rubble that lay within a depression where the dug-out basement had been. On the western lip of the hollow grew a tangle of once-cultivated lilac bushes now gone wild and untidy, some of them mere dead sticks, others alive but tall and rangy, in season showing but scant blooms.

Wa did not know of the existence of this place, yet ten minutes after climbing the ridge he led us directly to the untidy clearing and aimed himself straight as an arrow at the clump of lilacs, his sister, as before, dogging him. Thinking that no harm could come to them here, I stopped at the edge of the trees and let them cross the intervening seventy-five yards on their own. But because I was extremely interested in Wa's reasons, if indeed he had any, for heading in this direction, I lifted the field glasses and scanned the area ahead, focusing first on the lilacs, afterward sweeping the more open ground all the way to the forest on the other side, a matter of two hundred yards. Apart from a few birds and a number of insects, I saw nothing that could have accounted for Wa's singular behavior. The cubs reached the lilacs, and Wa went into them and led the way to the depression beyond. I started walking, but was only halfway to the lilac bushes when the agonized screams of both pups galvanized me into a full run, my stomach contracting with fear.

Running around the lilacs, I literally jumped into the hollow to discover both cubs blundering around in frantic circles as they pawed at their muzzles.

The porcupine was even then climbing sluggishly up the bank, heading toward the lilac bushes, the only refuge around the place, his club of a tail lashing jerkily from side to side, his muttering voice, like the grumble of a toothless, aged man, audible above the yelping of the pups. I grabbed for Matta first because she happened to stumble toward me, but when I saw that only one yellow quill was stuck fast at the very end of her nose, I let her go while I went to check Wa. He avoided me at first, made too frantic by the burning quills to realize that rescue was at hand. Matta, meanwhile, was following me, crying pitifully. Again I turned to her, held her head with my left hand, and grasped the quill firmly between thumb and forefinger of my right. I gave a quick, sharp pull. The quill, buried in her flesh to a depth of a quarter of an inch, came out with that rasping feel with which I was personally familiar; a gout of carmine blood seeped out. Matta stilled her screams, whimpering softly instead.

I managed to grab Wa a few moments later and was much relieved to see that though he had collected three quills, only one was properly embedded. Two dangled loosely from the top of his nose, like badly placed *banderillas* in the back of a *Muira* bull; the bad one was in his cheek, only two inches below his right eye; it appeared to have penetrated to a depth of half an inch. I pulled out the two loose barbs and tried to extricate the deep one, but it kept slipping through my finger, pouching Wa's cheek at each jerk. The cub, naturally, shrieked the louder every time I pulled. In the end I bent down, put my face close to his, holding his head still with both hands, and grasped the end of the quill between my front teeth. The serrated point let go in response to the yank that I gave, and the usual red goutlet blossomed on Wa's face. He gave a great shriek when the thing came out, but the immediate relief that followed transformed the cry into a whimper. Since my own flesh had been similarly punctured several times in the past, I knew exactly how my wards felt.

I called them to me, climbing the opposite edge of the hollow, where I sat and cradled them both, stroking them and speaking soothingly. They became quiet; soon they stopped shivering.

While this was going on, the porcupine, after attaining the highest point possible, clung to a spindly lilac trunk about seven feet from the ground and stared at us in myopic apprehension. The creature did not feel safe so close to the enemy; it would have much preferred a tall tree, it seemed to say with its husky, muttering voice.

When first Wa and then Matta recovered most of their equanimity, and bearing in mind the need to drive home the lesson, I got up and sought to lead them toward the lilacs, intending to growl warningly when we got close. I didn't have to. Neither cub would allow itself to be led anywhere near the porcupine, and when I carried them back down into the hollow, then set them on their feet, they scrambled hastily up the bank and started to run toward the distant trees, causing me to chase after them and to call until they at last stopped and waited for me a good hundred yards away. The lesson had been well and truly learned. Henceforth, they avoided even the scent of old porcupine droppings, and when, that winter, I was forced to execute one of the prickly fellows whom I discovered one morning breakfasting on the bark of one of our healthiest and most spectacular elm trees, the wolves, now almost full grown, would not come near the cadaver; neither would Tundra.

Homeward bound after the scare, Matta and Wa were subdued, following close to my heels as we retraced our route. I gave long and serious consideration to Wa's inexplicable behavior, tempted to believe that the young wolf was able to scent the porcupine from a distance of more than a mile but not daring to entirely accept such an incredible conclusion. Yet no other presented itself for scrutiny, unless the cub had been initially motivated by some different odor or sound and was drawn to the hollow only after getting closer to it and catching the porcupine's scent. I gave up trying to solve the puzzle in the end. It was to remain unsolved.

Matta and Wa had been exceedingly fortunate to escape so lightly from an encounter with a porcupine. Perhaps their agility contributed to their narrow escape, but luck, it seemed to me, was the main agent of their deliverance. The barbs removed from their faces were the shorter, thicker quills from the porcupine's tail, which evidently had brushed lightly against both cubs at the same time. I was prompted to this conclusion by the fact that if one had been harpooned before the other, the unscathed cub would have backed away when its sibling screamed in agony. I shuddered to think what would have happened if one or both pups had taken a full smash in the face from the lethal tail. Nevertheless, since the fracas had ended so well, I was glad that the incident had taken place. It was an excellent lesson for the cubs.

CHAPTER FOUR

Good Old Uncle Albert

FARLEY MOWAT

FARLEY MOWAT *was born in Belleville, Ontario,
in 1921 and grew up in Ontario and Saskatchewan.
He received his bachelor of arts degree from the University
of Toronto and has been awarded honorary doctorates from
numerous Canadian universities. His stories of nature and
of the Canadian Arctic have made him one of the most
popular writers in Canada. "I am a Northern Man,"
he says. "I like to think I am a reincarnation of the Norse
saga men and, like them, my chief concern is with the tales
of men, and other animals, living under conditions of
natural adversity." His best-selling books include* People
of the Deer *(1952),* The Dog Who Wouldn't Be
(1957), The Desperate People *(1959),* The Boat
Who Wouldn't Float *(1981),* A Whale for the Killing *(1984), and dozens of others. He is the recipient of
the Governor-General's Award, the Anisfield-Wolf
Award, the Canadian Authors Award, the Book
of the Year Medal, the Mark Twain Award,
and many other honors.*

MY PRECAUTIONS against disturbing the wolves were
superfluous. It had required a week for me to get their
measure, but they must have taken mine at our first
meeting; and, while there was nothing overtly disdain-
ful in their evident assessment of me, they managed to
ignore my presence, and indeed my very existence, with
a thoroughness which was somehow disconcerting.

Quite by accident I had pitched my tent within ten

yards of one of the major paths used by the wolves when they were going to, or coming from, their hunting grounds to the westward; and only a few hours after I had taken up residence one of the wolves came back from a trip and discovered me and my tent. He was at the end of a hard night's work and was clearly tired and anxious to go home to bed. He came over a small rise fifty yards from me with his head down, his eyes half-closed, and a preoccupied air about him. Far from being the preternaturally alert and suspicious beast of fiction, this wolf was so self-engrossed that he came straight on to within fifteen yards of me, and might have gone right past the tent without seeing it at all, had I not banged my elbow against the teakettle, making a re-sounding clank. The wolf's head came up and his eyes opened wide, but he did not stop or falter in his pace. One brief, sidelong glance was all he vouchsafed to me as he continued on his way.

It was true that I wanted to be inconspicuous, but I felt uncomfortable at being so totally ignored. Never-theless, during the two weeks which followed, one or more wolves used the track past my tent almost every night—and never, except on one memorable occasion, did they evince the slightest interest in me.

By the time this happened I had learned a good deal about my wolfish neighbors, and one of the facts which had emerged was that they were not nomadic roamers, as is almost universally believed, but were settled beasts and the possessors of a large permanent estate with very definite boundaries.

The territory owned by my wolf family comprised

more than a hundred square miles, bounded on one side by a river but otherwise not delimited by geographical features. Nevertheless there *were* boundaries, clearly indicated in wolfish fashion.

Anyone who has observed a dog doing his neighborhood rounds and leaving his personal mark on each convenient post will have already guessed how the wolves marked out *their* property. Once a week, more or less, the clan made the rounds of the family lands and freshened up the boundary markers—a sort of lupine beating of the bounds. This careful attention to property rights was perhaps made necessary by the presence of two other wolf families whose lands abutted on ours, although I never discovered any evidence of bickering or disagreements between the owners of the various adjoining estates. I suspect, therefore, that it was more of a ritual activity.

In any event, once I had become aware of the strong feeling of property rights which existed amongst the wolves, I decided to use this knowledge to make them at least recognize my existence. One evening, after they had gone off for their regular nightly hunt, I staked out a property claim of my own, embracing perhaps three acres, with the tent at the middle, and *including a hundred-yard-long section of the wolves' path.*

Staking the land turned out to be rather more difficult than I had anticipated. In order to ensure that my claim would not be overlooked, I felt obliged to make a property mark on stones, clumps of moss, and patches of vegetation at intervals of not more than fifteen feet around the circumference of my claim. This took most of the night and required frequent returns to the tent to consume copious quantities of tea; but before dawn brought the hunters home the task was done, and I retired, somewhat exhausted, to observe results.

I had not long to wait. At 0814 hours, according to my wolf log, the leading male of the clan appeared over the ridge behind me, padding homeward with his usual air of preoccupation. As usual he did not deign to glance at the tent; but when he reached the point where my property line intersected the trail, he stopped as abruptly as if he had run into an invisible wall. He was only fifty yards from me and with my binoculars I could see his expression very clearly.

His attitude of fatigue vanished and was replaced by a look of bewilderment. Cautiously he extended his nose and sniffed at one of my marked bushes. He did not seem to know what to make of it or what to do about it. After a minute of complete indecision he backed away a few yards and sat down. And then, finally, he looked directly at the tent and at me. It was a long, thoughtful, considering sort of look.

Having achieved my object—that of forcing at least one of the wolves to take cognizance of my existence— I now began to wonder if, in my ignorance, I had transgressed some unknown wolf law of major importance and would have to pay for my temerity. I found myself regretting the absence of a weapon as the look I was getting became longer, yet more thoughtful, and still more intent.

I began to grow decidedly fidgety, for I dislike staring matches, and in this particular case I was up against a master, whose yellow glare seemed to become more baleful as I attempted to stare him down.

The situation was becoming intolerable. In an effort to break the impasse I loudly cleared my throat and turned my back on the wolf (for a tenth of a second) to indicate as clearly as possible that I found his continued scrutiny impolite, if not actually offensive.

He appeared to take the hint. Getting to his feet he had another sniff at my marker, and then he seemed to make up his mind. Briskly, and with an air of decision, he turned his attention away from me and began a systematic tour of the area I had staked out as my own. As he came to each boundary marker he sniffed it once or twice, then carefully placed *his* mark on the outside of each clump of grass or stone. As I watched I saw where I, in my ignorance, had erred. He made his mark with such economy that he was able to complete the entire circuit without having to reload once, or, to change the simile slightly, he did it all on one tank of fuel.

The task completed—and it had taken him no longer than fifteen minutes—he rejoined the path at the point where it left my property and trotted off towards his home—leaving me with a good deal to occupy my thoughts.

■

Once it had been formally established, and its existence ratified by the wolves themselves, my little enclave in their territory remained inviolate. Never again did a wolf trespass on my domain. Occasionally, one in passing would stop to freshen up some of the boundary marks on his side of the line, and, not to be outdone in ceremony, I followed suit to the best of my ability. Any lingering doubts I might have had as to my personal safety dissolved, and I was free to devote all my attention to the study of the beasts themselves.

Very early in my observations I discovered that they led a well-regulated life, although they were not slavish adherents to fixed schedules. Early in the evenings the males went off to work. They might depart at four o'clock or they might delay until six or seven, but sooner or later off they went on the nightly hunt. During this hunt they ranged far afield, although always— as far as I could tell—staying within the limits of the family territory. I estimated that during a normal hunt they covered thirty or forty miles before dawn. When times were hard they probably covered even greater distances, since on some occasions they did not get home until the afternoon. During the balance of the daylight hours they slept—but in their own peculiarly wolfish way, which consisted of curling up for short wolf-naps of from five to ten minutes' duration; after each of which they would take a quick look about, and then turn round once or twice before dozing off again.

The females and the pups led a more diurnal life. Once the males had departed in the evening, the female usually went into the den and stayed there, emerging only occasionally for a breath of air, a drink, or sometimes for a visit to the meat cache for a snack.

This cache deserves special mention. No food was ever stored or left close to the den; and only enough was brought in at one time for immediate consumption. Any surplus from a hunt was carried to the cache, which was located in a jumble of boulders half-a-mile from the den, and stuffed into crevices, primarily for the use of the nursing female who, of course, could not join the male wolves on extended hunting trips.

The cache was also used surreptitiously by a pair of foxes who had their own den close by. The wolves must have known of the location of the foxes' home, and probably knew perfectly well that there was a certain amount of pilfering from their cache; but they did nothing about it even though it would have been a simple matter for them to dig out and destroy the litter of fox pups. The foxes, on their side, seemed to have no fear of the wolves, and several times I saw one flit like a shadow across the esker within a few yards of a wolf without eliciting any response.

Later I concluded that almost all the dens used by the Barren Land wolves were abandoned fox burrows which had been taken over and enlarged by the wolves. It is possible that the usefulness of the foxes as preliminary excavators may have guaranteed them immunity; but it seems more likely that the wolves' tolerance simply reflected their general amiability.

During the day, while the male wolves took it easy, the female would be reasonably active about her household chores. Emerging boisterously from the close confines of the den, the pups also became active—to the point of total exhaustion. Thus throughout the entire twenty-four-hour period there was usually something going on, or at least the expectation of something, to keep me glued to the telescope.

After the first two days and nights of nearly continuous observing I had about reached the limits of my endurance. It was a most frustrating situation. I did not dare to go to sleep for fear of missing something vital. On the other hand, I became so sleepy that I was seeing double, if not triple, on occasion; although this effect may have been associated with the quantities of wolf-juice which I consumed in an effort to stay awake.

I saw that something drastic would have to be done or my whole study program would founder. I could think of nothing adequate until, watching one of the males dozing comfortably on a hillock near the den, I recognized the solution to my problem. It was simple. I had only to learn to nap like a wolf.

It took some time to get the knack of it. I experimented by closing my eyes and trying to wake up again five minutes later, but it didn't work. After the first two or three naps I failed to wake up at all until several hours had passed.

The fault was mine, for I had failed to imitate *all* the actions of a dozing wolf, and, as I eventually discovered, the business of curling up to start with, and spinning about after each nap, was vital to success. I don't know why this is so. Perhaps changing the position of the body helps to keep the circulation stimulated. I *do* know, however, that a series of properly conducted wolf-naps is infinitely more refreshing than the unconscious coma of seven or eight hours' duration which represents the human answer to the need for rest.

Unfortunately, the wolf-nap does not readily lend itself to adaptation into our society, as I discovered after my return to civilization when a young lady of whom

I was enamored at the time parted company with me. She had rather, she told me vehemently, spend her life with a grasshopper who had rickets, than spend one more night in bed with me.

■

As I grew more completely attuned to their daily round of family life I found it increasingly difficult to maintain an impersonal attitude toward the wolves. No matter how hard I tried to regard them with scientific objectivity, I could not resist the impact of their individual personalities. Because he reminded me irresistibly of a Royal Gentleman for whom I worked as a simple soldier during the war, I found myself calling the father of the family George, even though in my notebooks, he was austerely identified only as Wolf "A."

George was a massive and eminently regal beast whose coat was silver-white. He was about a third larger than his mate, but he hardly needed this extra bulk to emphasize his air of masterful certainty. George had presence. His dignity was unassailable, yet he was by no means aloof. Conscientious to a fault, thoughtful of others, and affectionate within reasonable bounds, he was the kind of father whose idealized image appears in many wistful books of human family reminiscences, but whose real prototype has seldom paced the earth upon two legs. George was, in brief, the kind of father every son longs to acknowledge as his own.

His wife was equally memorable. A slim, almost pure-white wolf with a thick ruff around her face, and wide-spaced, slightly slanted eyes, she seemed the picture of a minx. Beautiful, ebullient, passionate to a degree, and devilish when the mood was on her, she hardly looked like the epitome of motherhood; yet there could have been no better mother anywhere. I found myself calling her Angeline, although I have never been able to trace the origin of that name in the murky depths of my own subconscious. I respected and liked George very much, but I became deeply fond of Angeline, and still live in hopes that I can somewhere find a human female who embodies all her virtues.

Angeline and George seemed as devoted a mated pair as one could hope to find. As far as I could tell they never quarreled, and the delight with which they greeted each other after even a short absence was obviously unfeigned. They were extremely affectionate with one another, but, alas, the many pages in my notebook which had been hopefully reserved for detailed comments on the sexual behavior and activities of wolves remained obstinately blank as far as George and Angeline were concerned.

Distressing as it was to my expectations, I discovered that physical lovemaking enters into the lives of a pair of mated wolves only during a period of two or three weeks early in the spring, usually in March. Virgin females (and they are all virginal until their second year) then mate; but unlike dogs, who have adopted many of the habits of their human owners, wolf bitches mate with only a single male, and mate for life.

Whereas the phrase "till death us do part" is one of the more amusing mockeries in the nuptial arrangements of a large proportion of the human race, with wolves it is a simple fact. Wolves are also strict monogamists, and although I do not necessarily consider this an admirable trait, it does make the reputation for unbridled promiscuity which we have bestowed on the wolf somewhat hypocritical.

While it was not possible for me to know with exact certainty how long George and Angeline had been mated, I was later able to discover from Mike that they had been together for at least five years—or the equivalent of thirty years in terms of the relative longevity of wolves and men. Mike and the Eskimos recognized the wolves in their area as familiar individuals, and the Eskimos (but not Mike) held the wolves in such high regard that they would not have thought of killing them or doing them an injury. Thus not only were George, Angeline and other members of the family well known to the Eskimos, but the site of their den had been known for some forty or fifty years, during which time generations of wolves had raised families there.

■

One factor concerning the organization of the family mystified me very much at first. During my early visit to the den I had seen *three* adult wolves; and during the first few days of observing the den I had again glimpsed the odd-wolf-out several times. He posed a major conundrum, for while I could accept the idea of a contented domestic group consisting of mated male and female and a bevy of pups, I had not yet progressed far enough into the wolf world to be able to explain, or to accept, the apparent existence of an eternal triangle.

Whoever the third wolf was, he was definitely a character. He was smaller than George, not so lithe and vigorous, and with a gray overcast to his otherwise white coat. He became "Uncle Albert" to me after the first time I saw him with the pups.

The sixth morning of my vigil had dawned bright and sunny, and Angeline and the pups took advantage of the good weather. Hardly was the sun risen (at three A.M.) when they all left the den and adjourned to a nearby sandy knoll. Here the pups worked over their mother with an enthusiasm which would certainly have driven any human female into hysterics. They were hungry; but they were also full to the ears with hellery. Two of them did their best to chew off Angeline's tail, worrying it and fighting over it until I thought I could actually see her fur flying like spindrift; while the other two did what they could to remove her ears.

Angeline stood it with noble stoicism for about an hour and then, sadly disheveled, she attempted to protect herself by sitting on her tail and tucking her mauled head down between her legs. This was a fruitless effort. The pups went for her feet, one to each paw, and I was treated to the spectacle of the demon killer of the wilds trying desperately to cover her paws, her tail, and her head at one and the same instant.

Eventually she gave it up. Harassed beyond endurance she leaped away from her brood and raced to the top of a high sand ridge behind the den. The four pups rolled cheerfully off in pursuit, but before they could reach her she gave vent to a most peculiar cry.

The whole question of wolf communications was to intrigue me more and more as time went on, but on this occasion I was still laboring under the delusion that complex communications among animals other than man did not exist. I could make nothing definite of Angeline's high-pitched and yearning whine-cum-howl. I did, however, detect a plaintive quality in it which made my sympathies go out to her.

I was not alone. Within seconds of her *cri-de-coeur,* and before the mob of pups could reach her, a savior appeared.

It was the third wolf. He had been sleeping in a bed hollowed in the sand at the southern end of the esker where it dipped down to disappear beneath the waters of the bay. I had not known he was there until I saw his head come up. He jumped to his feet, shook himself, and trotted straight toward the den—intercepting the pups as they prepared to scale the last slope to reach their mother.

I watched, fascinated, as he used his shoulder to bowl the leading pup over on its back and send it skidding down the lower slope toward the den. Having broken the charge, he then nipped another pup lightly on its fat behind; then he shepherded the lot of them back to what I later came to recognize as the playground area.

I hesitate to put human words into a wolf's mouth, but the effect of what followed was crystal clear. "If it's a workout you kids want," he might have said, "then I'm your wolf!"

And so he was. For the next hour he played with the pups with as much energy as if he were still one himself. The games were varied, but many of them were quite recognizable. Tag was the standby, and Albert was always "it." Leaping, rolling and weaving amongst the pups, he never left the area of the nursery knoll, while at the same time leading the youngsters such a chase that they eventually gave up.

Albert looked them over for a moment and then, after a quick glance toward the crest where Angeline was now lying in a state of peaceful relaxation, he flung himself in among the tired pups, sprawled on his back, and invited mayhem. They were game. One by one they roused and went into battle. They were really roused this time, and no holds were barred—by them, at any rate.

Some of them tried to choke the life out of Albert, although their small teeth, sharp as they were, could never have penetrated his heavy ruff. One of them, in an excess of infantile sadism, turned its back on him and pawed a shower of sand into his face. The others took to leaping as high into the air as their bowed little legs would propel them; coming down with a satisfying thump on Albert's vulnerable belly. In between jumps they tried to chew the life out of whatever vulnerable parts came to tooth.

I began to wonder how much he could stand. Evidently he could stand a lot, for not until the pups were totally exhausted and had collapsed into complete somnolence did he get to his feet, careful not to step on the small, sprawled forms, and disengage himself. Even then he did not return to the comfort of his own bed (which he had undoubtedly earned after a night of hard hunting) but settled himself instead on the edge of the nursery knoll, where he began wolf-napping, taking a quick look at the pups every few minutes to make sure they were still safely near at hand.

His true relationship to the rest of the family was still uncertain; but as far as I was concerned he had become, and would remain, "good old Uncle Albert."

CHAPTER FIVE

The East Fork Wolves

ADOLPH MURIE

ADOLPH MURIE *was born in 1899, the son of
Norwegian immigrants to the United States. He graduated from the Concordia College in Moorhead, Minnesota, and later received a doctorate from the University of
Michigan. He first went to Alaska in 1922 to help his
stepbrother Olaus in biological studies of caribou. In 1939
he began a two-year study of wolves that resulted in his
classic* The Wolves of Mount McKinley *(1944). In
that book, he concluded that "wolf predation probably has
a salutary effect on the (Dall) Sheep as a species," a view
that was contrary to popular opinion at the time. He held
strong views on the study of wildlife, preferring non-
intrusive methods to those that disturbed or altered the
animals' behavior. In 1963, he was awarded the
John Burroughs Medal for his book* A Naturalist
in Alaska *(1961). He died in 1974.*

IN FRONT OF OUR CABIN at East Fork River, on May
15, 1940, wolf tracks were seen in the fresh snow cov-
ering the gravel bars. The tracks led in both directions,
but since there was no game upstream at the time to
attract the wolves, it appeared that some other interest,
which I hoped was a den, accounted for their movement
that way. I followed the tracks up the bar for a mile and
a half directly to the den on a point of the high bank
bordering the river bed. In contrast to the Toklat den,
which was located in the woods in a flat patch of timber, this one was 2 miles beyond the last scraggly tim-

39

ber, on an open point about 100 feet above the river where the wolves had an excellent view of the surrounding country. Apparently a variety of situations are chosen for dens for I was told of two others which were located in timber, and of a third which was in a treeless area at the head of a dry stream.

Foxes had dug the original den on the point, and wolves had later moved in and had enlarged a few of the burrows. It seems customary in this region for wolves to preempt fox dens. Former Ranger Swisher, who had found at least four wolf dens, said that all of them had originally been dug by foxes. There are many unoccupied fox dens available so it is not strange that they are generally used by the wolves. The soil at the sites is sandy or loamy, at least free of rocks, so that digging is easy. Only a little enlarging of one of the many burrows is required to make a den habitable for a wolf. Although the adult wolves can only use the enlarged burrow, the whole system of burrows is available to the pups for a few weeks. This advantage is incidental and probably has no bearing on the choice of fox dens as homes.

When I approached this den a black male wolf was resting 70 yards away. He ran off about a quarter of a mile or less and howled and barked at intervals. As I stood 4 yards from the entrance, the female furtively pushed her head out of the burrow, then withdrew it, but in a moment came out with a rush, galloped most of the way down the slope, and stopped to bark at me. Then she galloped toward the male hidden in a ravine, and both parents howled and barked until I left.

From the den I heard the soft whimpering of the pups. It seemed I had already intruded too far, enough to cause the wolves to move. As I could not make matters much worse, I wriggled into the burrow which was 16 inches high and 25 inches wide. Six feet from the entrance of the burrow there was a right angle turn. At the turn there was a hollow, rounded and worn, which obviously was a bed much used by an adult. Due to the melting snow it was full of water in which there was a liberal sprinkling of porcupine droppings. A porcupine had used the place the preceding winter. Its feeding signs had been noted on the many nearby willows. From the turn the burrow slanted slightly upward for 6 feet to the chamber in which the pups were huddled and squirming. With a hooked willow I managed to pull three of the six pups to me. Not wishing to subject all of them to even a slight wetting, and feeling guilty about disturbing the den so much, I withdrew with the three I had. Their eyes were closed and they appeared to be about a week old. They were all females, and dark, almost black. One appeared slightly lighter than the other two and I placed her in my packsack to keep for closer acquaintance. [The pup was raised by Murie.] The other two were returned to their chamber and I departed.

After my intrusion it seemed certain that the family would move, so the following morning I walked toward the den to take up their trail before the snow melted. But from a distance I saw the black male curled up on the point 15 yards from the entrance, so it was apparent that they had not moved away after all. In fact, they remained at the den until the young were old enough to move off with the adults at the normal time.

On a ridge across the river from the den, about a half mile or less away, there were excellent locations for watching the wolves without disturbing them. There was also a view of the landscape for several miles in all directions.

Between May 15, when the den was discovered, and July 7, when the wolves moved a mile away, I spent about 195 hours observing them. The longest continuous vigil was 33 hours, and twice I observed them all night. Frequently I watched a few hours in the evening to see the wolves leave for the night hunt. Late in the summer and in the early fall after the family had left the den, I had the opportunity on a few occasions to watch the family for several hours at a time.

So far as I am aware it has been taken for granted that a wolf family consists of a pair of adults and pups. Perhaps that is the rule, although we may not have enough information about wolves to really know. Usually when a den is discovered the young are destroyed and all opportunity for making further observations is thereby lost.

The first week after finding the East Fork den I remained away from its vicinity to let the wolves regain whatever composure they had lost when I intruded in their home. On May 25, a few days after beginning an almost daily watch of the den, I was astonished at seeing two strange gray wolves move from where they had been lying a few yards from the den entrance. These two gray wolves proved to be males. They rested at the den most of the day. At 4 P.M., in company with the black father wolf, they departed for the night hunt. Because I had not watched the den closely the first week after finding it I do not know when the two gray males first made their appearance there, but judging from later events it seems likely that they were there occasionally from the first.

Five days later, a second black wolf—a female—was seen, making a total of five adults at the den—three males and two females. These five wolves lounged at the den day after day until the family moved away. There may have been another male in the group for I learned that a male had been inadvertently shot about 2 miles from the den a few days before I found the den.

Late in July another male was seen with the band, and a little later a fourth extra male joined them. These seven wolves, or various combinations of them, were frequently seen together in August and September. Five of the seven were males. The four extra males appeared to be bachelors.

The relationship of the two extra males and the extra female to the pair is not known. They may have been pups born to the gray female in years past or they may have been her brothers and sister, or no blood relation at all. I knew the gray female in 1939. She was then traveling with two gray and two black wolves which I did not know well enough to be certain they were the same as those at the den in 1940. But since the color combination of the wolves traveling together was the same in 1940 as in 1939, it is quite certain that the same wolves were involved. So apparently all the adult wolves at the den in 1940 were at least 2 years old. In 1941 it was known that the extra male with the female was at least 2 years old for he was an easily identified gray male which was at the den in 1940. The fact that none of the 1940 pups was at the 1941 den supports the conclusion that the extra wolves at the 1940 den were not the previous year's pups.

The presence of the five adults in the East Fork family during denning time in 1940 and three in 1941, and three adults in the Savage River family, suggests that it may not be uncommon to find more than two adults at a den. The presence of extra adults is an unusual family make-up which is probably an outcome of the close association of the wolves in the band. It should be an advantage for the parents to have help in hunting and feeding the pups.

Wolves vary much in color, size, contour, and action. No doubt there is also much variation in temperament. Many are so distinctively colored or patterned that they can be identified from afar. I found the gray ones more easily identified since among them there is more individual variation in color pattern than in the black wolves.

The mother of the pups was dark gray, almost "bluish," over the back, and had light under parts, a blackish face, and a silvery mane. She was thick-bodied, short-legged, short-muzzled, and smaller than the others. She was easily recognized from afar.

The father was black with a yellowish vertical streak behind each shoulder. From a distance he appeared coal black except for the yellow shoulder marks, but a nearer view revealed a scattering of silver and rusty hairs, especially over the shoulders and along the sides. There was an extra fullness of the neck under the chin. He seemed more solemn than the others, but perhaps that was partly imagined by me, knowing as I did that many of the family cares rested on his shoulders. On the hunts that I observed he usually took the lead in running down caribou calves.

The other black wolf was a slender-built, long-legged female. Her muzzle seemed exceptionally long, reminding me of the Little Red Riding Hood illustrations. Her neck was not as thick as that of the black male. This female had no young in 1940, but had her own family in 1941.

What appeared to be the largest wolf was a tall, rangy male with a long silvery mane and a dark mantle over the back and part way down over the sides. He seemed to be the lord and master of the group although he was not mated to any of the females. The other wolves approached this one with some diffidence, usually cowering before him. He deigned to wag his tail only after the others had done so. He was also the dandy in appearance. When trotting off for a hunt his tail waved jauntily and there was a spring and sprightly spirit in his step. The excess energy at times gave him a rocking-horse gallop quite different from that of any of the others.

The other gray male at the den I called "Grandpa" in my notes. He was a rangy wolf of a nondescript color. There were no distinctive markings, but he moved as though he were old and a little stiff. Sometimes he had sore feet which made him limp. From all appearances he was an old animal, although in this I may be mistaken.

One of the grays that joined the group in late July was a large male with a light face except for a black robber's mask over the eyes. His chest was conspicuously white. He moved with much spring and energy. The black mask was distinctive and recognizable from a distance.

The other wolf, which joined the group in August, was a huge gray animal with a light yellowish face. In 1941 he was mated to the small black female which had no young the preceding year.

All these wolves could be readily distinguished within the group but some of the less distinctively marked ones might have been confused among a group of strange wolves. The black-faced gray female, the robber-masked male, and the black-mantled male were so characteristically marked that they could be identified in a large company.

CHAPTER SIX

Arctic Fall
LOIS CRISLER

LOIS CRISLER *was born in Spokane, Washington.
She was a teacher at the University of Washington before
marrying wildlife filmmaker Herb (Cris) Crisler.
The young couple spent a year and a half in the 1950s in
the Brooks Range of northern Alaska, where Cris fulfilled
an assignment to photograph the great caribou herds.
While in Alaska, they adopted a family of wild wolves
and discovered that the animals were not the vicious
killers of legend, but rather intelligent and highly
individualistic predators. The Crislers brought their wolves
back to Colorado with them at the conclusion of the film
assignment. The tragic conclusion to the lives of their
wolves was told by Lois Crisler in* Captive Wild,
published in 1968. She died in 1971.

"ON THE DECK," in the company only of arctic wolves, we faced the most dramatic event of our lives so far, the approach of arctic winter. The land sometimes wore a look we called the "mystic-arctic look." The first storm of fall had that look, and the inner and haunting menace that gave it the mystic quality.

You could hardly call it a storm; it was simply an inimical condition. There was grayness in the air and the whuff of wind forever around the crackerbox. The most strange, unnerving fact was that the blurred sun was present but unfriending. It seemed—and not merely as a figure of speech—to have gone under a spell. It looked down upon a dead, nonmortal land, vacant and enormous, from which all small forms of life had gone in or away.

The mystic-arctic look took many forms. It appeared one still, gray afternoon when we camera-hunted a high ridge, filming at f 2 in the dark light. Twice the hidden sun spotlighted a cradle of land far off in the tundra below, gilding it. We stood looking down at the many waters—ponds, lakes, rivers, all gray—at the dim arctic mountains and that cradle of light. Merely as a statement of fact, Cris said, "Out of this world, isn't it!"

A haunting thing happened as we neared home this day. From a draw came a caribou bull, trotting purposefully. He was the first caribou we had seen since moving into the crackerbox, though while we backpacked the lumber caribou bands had passed going north, fording with tantalizing picturesqueness; we had no time then for cameras.

The bull's face was proud and sullen. A last tag of velvet hung from the tip of one guard horn. His antlers were dry but still blood-tinged and grooved as for veins. He was stately in his fall coat. A bull's fall coat is magnificent—sleek brown back, deep underhang of white fur on the chest. To us he was only himself. He connected with nothing. But somewhere the big tide of migration was turning; this bull was a fleck of foam tossed ahead.

The oncoming of fall was slow. The climate north of the Range is arid, light snows came and went. But up on the mountains the grizzled whiteness moved evenly and inexorably toward our level.

The tundra froze leathery, thawed, then froze hard,

and our feet hit like iron one afternoon as we went, with five-gallon cans tied to our packboards, to bring water from the river. The spring near the mesa foot had frozen. The sun in the southwest, nearing the mountain-tops, was a marginless radiance. The brown tundra was covered with amber light, through which snow sped horizontally on a north wind from down the Killik. When there was a gust the myriad traveling flakes, widely separated, accelerated to streaks.

It stopped us—the amber light over the brown earth, filled with those speeding specks of white, the winding ice-rimmed river, the white mountains standing off on every side. "Did you ever see anything like it?" Cris said softly.

A wind drift formed behind each shrub but over all the tundra still looked brown. But this snow would not melt until spring.

We had a new feeling. It was the "arctic euphoria," which comes when the mighty landslide toward winter is irrevocable. We interpreted it in old ways. Cris said, unemphasized, with a shy quick glance at me, "I kind of like the challenge of the—unusual."

I cast my own exultation in terms I knew better than arctic ones—in forest terms. People are free and of equality in a wild sunlit wood, I thought. There is no criticism or grading by any usual standard. Not by clothes, money, manners, knowledge, heredity, power.

No man is slave, no man is master, facing the sunlight on wild wood and wild fur and eyes. Liberty seeps like health into your heart. The weight on your heart of being an object, being manipulated and having to strive cunningly—all that is lifted away. A wild shy honest delight steals into you. You breathe in a part of your being that had unconsciously been constricted.

All my life I had taken for granted I was free. Actually, these past months, I had for the first time been exposed to genuine freedom and it was just now beginning to take. There are feelings not specified. The accepted, labeled range of feelings is so small. Far, far around, the mountains and tundra were inviolate now and they said something to the heart.

■

Our wolves were growing up. They would reach about adult size by Christmas. Cris was as proud of their size and beauty as if he had achieved both by his own efforts.

"Isn't Trigger getting a fine big head!" he purred. "He looks like an executive. Their fur is so deep they don't touch the ground when they lie on it—like lying on a pincushion."

Their fur was not harsh. It was luxurious to bury your hands in, wealthy-deep with thick new undercoats of wool. Blond Trigger had darkened surprisingly with new black guard hairs.

Hardly anyone realizes what wolves look like. I know of only two artists, Olaus Murie and Bill Berry, who draw real wolves; the rest draw myth wolves, stocky and brutal-muzzled.

Real wolves are slender, invincibly aristocratic-looking. They have disarmingly sweet faces!

They are slender all over and as sinuous and graceful as cats. Bodies are long, and carried high on long legs. Paws and legs are unlike those of dogs. Legs are twined "nervously" with veins and sinews. (By nervous I mean innervated, alive and sensitive all over.) Paws are nervous too—not mere clumps like most dog paws, but long-fingered and spreading. Trigger's forepaw made a track as long and almost as spreading as that of my own long hand.

Beside a wolf, the most graceful dog looks wooden. Wolves seem to have a fineness and delicacy of articulation lost to dogs through centuries of breeding. In motion they ripple, they flow. Even in walking, the spine has a slight sidewise ripple.

And how wolves leap! Lifting leaps—straight up, all bushy and flowing, to the tip of the tail. Straight down. That is their way of participating in gaiety. They leap upward as if pulled at the shoulders by a skyhook. Or they leap perpendicular, standing straight up in air; that is the "observation leap." They leap sidewise. They leap backward. They twirl into a doughnut in midair and wind up the incredible act with a flourish—chest to ground, paws spread, and an inimitable, flashing wolf-toss of the head. Heads too are slender, long.

A wolf's most undoglike feature is his tail. He runs with his tail, thinks with it, marks mood with it, even controls with it. "They run with their tails as much as with their spines," observed Cris. The tail floats. The one position it never assumes is up and curled like a sled dog's tail.

We watched Lady think with her tail one day. She stood looking at a caribou skull, not really scared but skittish. She swirled and twirled her tail as a dubious squirrel will do.

The higher the wolf's spirits, the higher his tail. You glance at his tail to learn his mood. A typical tail position for a cheerful wolf is out an inch, then down. You can talk a gloomy wolf's tail into that position. Wolves are wonderfully responsive to a truly cheerful voice.

Since wolves have complete "differential relaxation," they don't wag their tails quite as dogs do. They wag them on about the same occasions but take the trouble to start only the base of the tail. The rest of the tail follows through, drifting languidly in a Delsarte gesture, the stump starting east while the tip drifts west. When the tail is not in use the wolf withdraws every ounce of residual tension; the tail hangs like a great tassel, subject only to wind and gravity.

On the other hand, wolves use their tails strongly and controllingly, like fifth arms. A wolf will flap his tail strongly over the back of another wolf running alongside. Legs are used the same way; that is, out at right angles. A wolf will lay not only a front leg but even a hind leg over the back of another wolf strongly and easily, as you would lay an arm. Also he can push backward hard with a forepaw. Strolling through a door he has just opened, he shoves it farther open behind him as you would do with your hand.

Undoglike too is his deep, narrow chest—deep from the side, narrow from the front, like the chest of a bull elk. A big male wolf may have less distance between the tops of his forelegs than a bulldog pup has. Not with any of the eight wolves we eventually knew could I insert my fingers flat together into that chest arch. I had to overlap them slightly.

Cris and I had a little ceremony every morning. It was going out to reap the wolves' morning welcome. We prized it so much we actually took turns. Wolves don't make a fuss over you any old time as dogs do.

I enjoyed their greeting of Cris almost as much as of me. I liked to hear his gruff pleasant voice as he undid the gate. "How's my little puppies?" The wolves danced and bowed along the inside of the fence. "Aren't they the nicest little wolves!"

He entered and the wolves all but knocked him down. Trigger stood up face to face, paws on Cris's chest, rough, heavy, beautiful, uttering a "half-howl" while Cris gently shook him by the furry jowls. Cris sat down on the ground. The wolves assaulted him from both sides and in a minute had him hunching his shoulders, giggling, gripping his cap down over his ears.

This was because Lady had invented a new game. She had stood up back of him one morning, forepaws on his shoulders, looking him over. (A wolf feels safer to approach from the rear for mischief.) She didn't want his fur collar; she didn't want his bandanna. Butt sharply forward she neatly untied with her teeth the strings holding up the ear flaps of his cap. From then on she untied them every time he sat down.

But still she was elusive; she would not let him hold her. She was quicksilver. She was a minx, a Cleopatra of changing moods. Trigger wanted to romp with Cris one morning. Obligingly Cris went for his gloves. But when he returned, Lady would not let Trigger touch him. She caught Trigger's tail, she bit his neck. He had to give his full attention to protecting himself.

"She's just made up her mind she won't let him play with me," said Cris.

He started from the pen, but this did not suit Lady either. She enticed him. She bowed, her eyes bright with mischief. But she still would not let him touch her. He turned back to Trigger.

At this Lady surrendered. She threw herself into Cris's arms, her pink tongue going in and out, trying to kiss his face, which he held back from her, laughing.

"You can't help f'm feeling flattered when a wolf plays with you," admitted Cris sheepishly.

He wanted to camera-hunt alone one morning but knew the wolves would want to go along. He waited in the little entry-way adjacent to the pen gate while I entered the pen to distract the wolves' attention. But they stood bright-eyed at the gate, relentlessly watching to spy that hidden figure.

"All right, all right," conceded Cris. "Let them go!"

Lady raced out radiant, rippling around the outside of the pen. Poor dignified Trigger stood bewildered. It wasn't walk time. Lady enticed him at the far end of the pen. She had taken a day's exercise already, racing around the willow bushes. Now she flowed back into the pen in one swift black invitation and smile. He followed her out.

And then the quality of happiness became visible, personified in Lady. She raced round and round the wood rick, leaping each time over the willow bushes at the end of it. Beyond the black wolf rose the smiling white morning mountains.

Big wolves are more exciting companions on the tundra than little wolves. The other wildings here were about the same as up in the pass during the summer: moose, grizzly, fox, caribou, wolves. But now Trigger and Lady could do something about them.

Lady gave Cris a scare the first time she saw as well as smelled a grizzly. She set out to chase it. If the grizzly took a notion to chase her, Cris knew she would head straight for him with the grizzly on her heels.

"Lady!" he yelled imperiously. The astounded grizzly reared to his hind legs. And back came Lady, but not purely from obedience.

She chased her first fox. She did her best but the fox toyed, not taking her seriously. When it saw she was gaining on it, the fox floated away. Foxes run faster than wolves. Another of those built-in governors on what wolves can do—like the speed differential between wolf and caribou.

Defeat made Lady morose. For a depressing companion commend me to a morose wolf.

Down on the sand bar one day she observed just the back of a moose moving along the high bank. She crouched and stalked as for sik-sik—parka squirrel. When she topped the bank and for the first time beheld the dimensions of a moose, she stood up, stopped trying to make herself small. She took a few faltering steps toward it. Then she turned and fled. She passed up Cris and me, hit the river at a bad deep place, plunged in regardless. On the far side, followed by Trigger, she disappeared into the willows.

Anxiously Cris headed homeward for his waders to cross and search for the wolves. Glancing back he saw them perched on the distant bank, their attention glued on the departing moose. "Not going to let that thing sneak up on them!" said Cris.

He blew his whistle and they came. But for hours afterward Lady felt glum. She snatched my whole hand in her mouth when I domineeringly continued to pet her after she warned me with a growl.

The wolves played one game so much we called it simply The Game. One wolf elected something—anything—as a trophy and ran with it, pursued by the other wolf.

Their other main game was pure histrionics. Down on the sand bars, where the matériel was easy, they played it. Never think wild animals don't enjoy ease. Lady would dig, look to see if Trigger was watching, then dig furiously, stopping to sniff the hole as if she had a mouse, until Trigger came over to see what she had. If he started a dig, each wolf tried to make the other come to his own dig. Usually Lady persisted till Trigger came to hers.

"She makes it look so-o-o attractive," said Cris.

In life-and-death affairs, as with the moose, the wolves asked no help from us. But they had one problem with which they felt our powers sufficed to deal. It was a social problem, and the last you would expect a wolf to have trouble with.

Lady came up to Cris on the walk one day, with an expression of distress and anxiety. She cried up to his face. It dawned on Cris what her trouble was: she had lost Trigger. He blew the whistle and Trigger came.

The next time this happened Cris failed to catch on. This time it was Trigger who had lost Lady and come crying to Cris. After appealing vainly to Cris, the wolf hurried back along the narrow slough between willows, down which we had just come.

Then here came Lady, crying too. Cris caught on. He pointed up the slough. "Trigger went that way," he stated briskly.

Lady looked up at his hand, up the slough, then away she went. "She understood perfectly," affirmed Cris with pride.

One day the wolves lost us. We were on the lake, shoveling a landing strip for Andy. Bored, the wolves ran off up the far mountainside. When ready to start for home, Cris blew the whistle. The wolves ran down the mountainside all right, but picked up their own trail and followed it back up the mountain.

My stomach felt sick and hit. What did they mean to do? Leave us? They were so far away up there that only Lady showed up; Trigger's silvery fur blended with the snow so that he all but vanished.

"Maybe they don't see us," Cris said. He led back from the willow tundra onto the white lake and whistled again. The wolves raced down the mountain as before. This time they streamed on toward us, getting bigger, tongues flapping, ears flattened, perfectly delighted to locate us.

When I had not gone along on the walks for a couple of days it was worth it to see Lady's joy when I did go. Over and over she ran back, dazzling-eyed, to spiral to the snow in the full wolf greeting, until the serious business of the tundra absorbed her—rabbits, voles, parka squirrels, ptarmigan, fox.

"I like to see Lady the way she was today," said Cris. "Squatting down in front, ears pinned back, eyes shining. She's so tickled you're going."

She gave me a great welcoming run one day that warms my heart yet. I had joined the walk late and Cris and the wolves were up on the mountainside. The wolves froze, watching, until I gave our "recognition sign," the crouch and arm-flip.

Back went Lady's ears. She came tearing down the mountainside, sailed right over the willow bushes, and threw herself at my feet in a cloud of powder snow, in the full wolf greeting. Trigger followed as usual.

You can't help sharing a wolf's joy.

CHAPTER SEVEN

At Home with the Arctic Wolf

DAVID MECH

*DAVID MECH received his bachelor's degree in conservation
from Cornell University and his doctorate in wildlife
ecology from Purdue University. He is widely regarded as
North America's foremost expert on the wolf and is the
author of hundreds of articles on wildlife topics. His book*
The Wolf: Ecology and Behavior of an Endangered
Species *(1970) is the classic textbook on wolf ecology.
He has served as chairman of the Wolf Specialist Group
of the International Union for the Conservation of Nature
and as consultant to the Northern Rocky Mountain Wolf
Recovery Team of the U.S. Fish & Wildlife Service.
He is now a wildlife research biologist with the U.S.
Fish & Wildlife Service and an adjunct professor
at the University of Minnesota.*

I HAD LITTLE IDEA how large the pack's territory was.
However, in Alaska, where there is much more prey,
wolf packs may range over a thousand square miles or
more, a radius of more than eighteen miles. I once
found my wolves fifteen miles from their den, returning
from a musk ox herd another two miles away, so probably their territory covered at least a thousand square
miles. It takes that much country to support enough
vulnerable prey—musk oxen and arctic hares primarily,
but also Peary caribou, ptarmigan, lemmings, seals,
and miscellaneous nesting birds.

Feeding six rapidly growing pups is a strenuous job,
and the pack devoted considerable time and effort to the

task. Part of the pack's basic schedule was to strike out each day on the hunt from about 3:30 to 10:00 P.M. on clear days, or 2:00 to 11:00 A.M. on overcast ones. My impression is that it was usually the pups, Scruffy, or Mom that aroused the rest of the pack from their half-day-long sleeps and urged them on.

July 23 was typical. About 2:40 A.M., when the whole pack was sprawled on a heathery hillside just east of the den ridge, Mom arose and strolled to each of the adults, nosing the males perfunctorily but fully arousing Mid-Back. After Mid-Back stood reluctantly for a minute or two, she settled back down. Mom headed northeast about one hundred feet, looked back at the immobile adults, sat, threw her head back, and began howling, faintly at first but eventually stimulating the pups.

No one could sleep through the resulting aural exuberance from the pack's peanut gallery. Six strained, intertwining strands of soprano yowling seemed to emphasize Mom's message: "We're hungry!" All the remaining pack members promptly joined the chorus, and the pups rushed them excitedly. Mom returned to the group, and the adults stiffly arose, stretched, socialized momentarily, and then followed Mom as she pranced off to the northeast on the nightly hunt.

On the other hand, most often Mom and/or Scruffy returned to the pups after a half hour and remained with them. Now I wish I had followed the pack several times to see at what point these animals broke away and returned. What were the circumstances? Did these babysitters decide on their own to return, or was it a group decision? Was there any coercion? Did Alpha Male play a role? Such questions remain to be answered, along with many others.

Take chorus howling, for instance. What is its role in the pack's social dynamics? One of my graduate students, Fred Harrington, and I studied howling in the Minnesota wolves and learned many of its functions. Fred recorded and analyzed hundreds of howls from my radioed wolf packs. Nevertheless, we still know no more about its role within the pack than when Lois Crisler wrote in *Arctic Wild* about the tame wolves she took to the Arctic and lived with: "Like a community sing, a howl is . . . a happy social occasion. Wolves love a howl."

I think we can eventually unravel the mystery of chorus howling with the High Arctic pack because it is so easy to observe the animals while recording their howling. And I have made a start. During 1986 alone, I noted group howling seventeen times. To generalize so far, the pack seems to howl on the following occasions: (1) when disturbed but not upset enough to flee, (2) when arising, (3) after intense playing or social interactions, and (4) when split up. The only common denominator among these situations seems to be arousal. But why must wolves howl when aroused?

Whatever the reason, pups pick up the trait early. Our pups howled the first day I found them, when about five weeks old. Certainly they could use howling to get attention, and I once saw a pup that had fallen a quarter mile behind the others return to the pack after a great deal of howling by the pup and the pack. Nevertheless, on another occasion, when a lone pup strayed a quarter mile from the den, Mom merely tracked it down and escorted it back without any vocalization.

Such observations are exactly the kind I had hoped to make when I first discovered the den, and I made far more than I ever anticipated. Some of the information I obtained was mundane. For example, the basic pack routine was sleep, bouts of play and social interaction lasting up to two hours, a daily hunt by most of the adults, and feeding of the pups whenever possible.

I never ceased to wonder about the amount and intensity of the pup's play. One day when about seven weeks old, the pups moved to an old snowfield about one hundred feet across in a depression on a hillside about a quarter mile up a valley from the den. For about forty-five minutes the pups scrambled back and forth across the snowfield, chasing one another, tackling, sliding, rolling, skidding, and carrying on to a degree I have never seen nor heard of before for any species. Sometimes they would pair up and wrestle like three tag teams on a snowy mat, and now and then Scruffy, who was really only an adult-sized pup himself, would rush in and attack the whole batch. Once he playfully grabbed one pup by the nape and hoisted its front quarters right off the snow.

Along with the intensive play, an occasional excursion, and the long hours of sleep, the pups' only other major activity was eating. They did that with great gusto as well. In fact, their basic feeding routine demanded gusto. To obtain most of their food, wolf pups must go through an elaborate ritual. As an adult approaches, especially one just returning after a long absence, the pups race each other to the animal, whining and wagging the entire rear halves of their bodies as they approach. When they meet the adult, they crouch and wag excitedly, hold their ears back, and lick rapidly at the mouth of the adult. Each competes frantically with the others in mobbing the adult and trying to get closest to the animal's mouth.

Usually the adult accepts the feverish solicitations for a few seconds, turns, and rushes away excitedly, weaving body and tail from side to side. The adult holds its head low, and the pups follow and try to continue mobbing its mouth. The adult may travel only a few feet or sometimes up to a quarter mile before stopping and suddenly regurgitating. The pups then frantically gobble up every bit of food that falls. Within less than thirty seconds, nothing is left. He or she who hesitates is truly lost.

This food-transfer process helps select for pups that are aggressive and large, and it increases any differences among pups: The rich get richer, the poor get poorer. This explains why in Minnesota I sometimes find litters in which some pups weigh twice as much as others.

The adult does not necessarily empty its stomach each time it feeds the pups, for during the next few hours, it may regurgitate two or three, or possibly more, times. Most often it was Mom or Scruffy who fed the pups, probably because these two spent the most time around the den where they could dig up food cached by the rest of the pack, and of course they were hounded the most by the pups. Nevertheless, I saw each of the other pack members, except Lone Ranger, re-gurgitate to the pups.

Although the main function of food begging and re-gurgitating is clearly to deliver food to the pups, there may be more to this interesting behavior than imme-diately apparent. I often saw adults competing with pups for food scraps lying around the den, yet after an adult succeeded in gobbling up the food, it would even-tually regurgitate to the pups. Because pups also devour pieces of prey brought to them directly, it is clear they do not need predigested food, so that does not seem to explain this behavior.

One possibility is that regurgitating food allows an adult to control when it grants the food to the pups, and asserting such control seems to be an important need. For example, I once watched Alpha Male regur-gitate to two pups. One immediately made off with a large chunk, while the other fed on the remaining pieces. The adult then growled at the pup and began re-eating the regurgitant. If he was training the pup to be competitive, it worked, for the pup quickly grabbed a chunk and fled with it.

On another occasion, Mid-Back, the pack's specialist in hare hunting, returned excitedly to the den area with a whole hare in her mouth. She strode rapidly by the other pack members, tail raised and hackles up. Scruffy ran to meet Mid-Back and escorted her solicitously as she headed to a favorite resting spot below the den it-self, lay down, and proceeded to flagrantly devour her catch. Scruffy lay beside her, groveled several times, and pawed fetchingly at her, and finally, just as the last stiff, furry hind foot was moving down Mid-Back's throat, he maneuvered directly in front of Mid-Back's head and slid his nose right up to the hare's foot in one last, desperate beg. The foot disappeared down Mid-Back's throat.

Question: Why didn't Mid-Back simply consume the hare where she had caught it and avoid all Scruffy's begging? Why deliver it to the den area with such flourish? Is there prestige, status, or some other social intangible to be gained by displaying one's catch? by regurgitating to the pups?

Certainly with food being so difficult to obtain, it might play an important role in pack relations, and social relations are extremely important to a wolf pack. They are the currency of the dominance hierarchy, which in turn sets the social structure of the pack, with top-ranking males and females, subordinates, and even "scape-wolves."

Other than the pack leader's position, which itself was not all that obvious, the other wolves' ranks on the social ladder took much watching for me to discern. The mother of the pups should have been a high-ranking wolf, but Mom often seemed to be the most submissive member of the pack, except perhaps for Scruffy. Among the adult males, there were few dominance interactions, and none of these animals was clearly Mom's mate.

Finally the answer dawned on me, or so I thought. No one has really had the chance to observe such interactions so close up before with a wild pack. Our present model for wolf social interactions is based primarily on captivity studies during the courtship and breeding season. What observations there have been of wild packs have been cursory, and most were made in winter. But this was midsummer. That is when the wolf's reproductive hormones are at their annual low. In short, it is a period of relative social peace. It might also be the time for an annual social reshuffle to begin. I was observing this social flux. The real contests, and those among the males, would not get underway until winter.

Possibly Mom had been the top female last year, so she got bred. However, as she devoted her energies and most of her food to the pups, she grew thinner and thinner. Such sacrifice would pay off for her genetically, for she would have six strong, healthy offspring to pass on her genes.

The only exception to the relative lack of dominance demonstrations I observed involved the pups. The adults were always "pinning" the pups, that is, forcing them to lie still with their necks to the ground. Why? Probably to constantly suppress the pervasive expansion tendency each wolf seems to be born with. It certainly was clear when the pups were away from the adults that each thought it could take over the world. Such an outlook would eventually be valuable when as an adult a wolf would have to routinely dart in and out among the thrashing hooves of a swirling herd of musk oxen. However, until such time, it would facilitate the pack's life if the pups just let the adults handle the important things.

The pups were constantly pinning each other, too.

Play fighting allows each pup to test and hone its competitive skills, and this is extremely important. Although pack functioning appears to be a model of cooperation, especially during the peaceful summer period, the basic selfish, competitive spirit of every living thing lurks constantly beneath. Nowhere was this more apparent than after the wolves made a kill.

From any high spot on the barren grounds I could scan hundreds of square miles. Musk oxen are dark and arctic hares white, and both usually travel in herds. Thus I was able to watch the wolves hunt both hares and musk oxen.

The most outstanding hare hunt I saw was very non-conventional. During early morning on July 25, I was making my usual nightly vigil from the hill immediately above and south of the den. I could see most of the wolves flopped out in the heather 150 feet downhill to the northeast. I could also view the activity area below, just west of the den, where a few hours before, I had watched Mid-Back tormenting Scruffy by devouring the hare before his very eyes. Across the valley to my left, a huge hill loomed a quarter mile away, covered on its side by the usual hummocks but smooth with gravel on top. It was just about 4:00 A.M., and the wolves had been flat since 1:30. My only excitement had come from swatting mosquitoes, which had discovered that since the previous day's snow had stopped, they could pester me without dodging snowflakes.

At 4:09 A.M., Mom suddenly looked up from her long snooze and stared momentarily at a white form a quarter mile away atop the big hill across the valley. She arose and trotted down the valley and up the hill straight toward what must be an adult hare. But surely the wolf didn't think she could ever catch the hare. It had all the advantages, being on top of the hill and able to intently watch the wolf approaching. Still the hare stuck tight as Mom labored over the hummocks and up the hill. Finally, when the wolf was about fifty yards away, the hare headed out.

"I told you so," I thought.

Mom made a token dash, slowed, and then nosed around where the hare had been. Suddenly the ground burst in front of her, and two or three young, gravel-colored hares sprang away. The wolf instantly chose the one streaking straight down hill and nabbed it at the bottom. Had the wolf seen these invisible hares from a quarter mile away? Or had she suspected they were there from the behavior of the adult?

With musk oxen, of course, the wolf's problem is not to catch them but to kill one without getting damaged itself. Males may weigh a half ton or more, and females half that, and they live in herds of up to thirty. When defending calves, adults squeeze together in a tight line or semicircle in front of the calves or in a circle with the calves inside. They have been known to kill wolves.

The problem in attempting to observe such tactics and how wolves try to overcome them was to get close enough to both musk oxen and wolves at the same time. Because it was far more fruitful for me to watch at the den than to try to keep up with the wolves while they scampered over the hummocks and up and down the hills on a hunt, my hopes began to fade. Until July 15, that is.

We had been watching at the den since 10:30 A.M. and had noticed a herd of eleven adult and three calf musk oxen below us a mile and a half away, approaching gradually from the east. The herd picked its way up and down the uneven terrain, scrounging the grasses and sedges that form their main summer diet. At times the herd would disappear in a depression, only to reappear in dark clumps here and there.

The wolves seemed pretty tired all day, and except for a short excursion with the pups 150 feet to the stream below and a play session there, little out of the ordinary happened. By 5:00 P.M., the musk oxen were only a mile away, so we busied ourselves observing them as well as the wolves, which were on the opposite side of the ridge we were watching from. Because the sky was perfectly clear, we expected the wolves to strike out on their hunt sometime in the evening.

"You know, Jim," I said, "if the wolves spot that herd and head down there, the whole thing might be over before we're packed up. What say we take a chance and get into position near the herd just in case?"

"Exactly what I've been thinking," the photographer replied. "The most we have to lose is a night's observation here, and we can make that up anytime."

It was one of our best decisions in this whole adventure. We immediately headed to the herd. The musk oxen were feeding and resting on a half-mile-wide plateau between two creeks. The terrain, while level, comprised hummocky polygon platforms some twenty to fifty feet wide, separated by troughs several feet across and a yard or so deep. Old bleached bones of a caribou and two disintegrating musk ox skulls perhaps hundreds of years old accented the sense of timelessness I felt in that proximity to the herd of shaggy beasts. Had I beamed back to the Stone Age?

Although we could glimpse wolves moving about on the den ridge a mile away, much of the route between the den and the musk oxen was obscured. However, soon after we positioned ourselves near the herd, some of the wolves seemed to be heading in our direction. Then they disappeared. About 7:30 P.M., all seven reappeared, threading their way diagonally down a hillside to our right; they had spotted the musk oxen! The wolves moved very deliberately, with little lingering, but at their usual five-mile-per-hour pace. They seemed interested but not too excited. Then I realized that this was nothing special for them. They see musk oxen every day.

But it certainly was special for me. I had observed only one other wolf encounter with musk oxen, just a week before, and it had been disappointing. The wolves had approached the herd and then lay down near it until distracted by a passing hare, which they spent the next half hour trying to catch. And that was it.

This time proved more exciting, although it started out basically the same as the other. The wolves approached the herd quite casually, and the musk oxen tightened and faced them. Each adult ox continually shifted its rear end around slightly, pressing against its neighbor. The wolves stood and watched ten feet away, with Scruffy hanging back a few feet. After several minutes, most wolves lay down, although now and then individuals got up and walked around. They did not seem excited.

The musk oxen, however, took the situation seriously. They stood facing their adversaries, heads lowered and calves huddled at their rumps. Nevertheless they appeared disorganized. Single oxen on the edges eventually broke rank, and some seemed more interested in eating. Neither did the wolves have it all together. At one point, Scruffy and one of the adult males started strolling away from the musk oxen while another adult male on the other side of the herd challenged the beasts.

As the casual confrontation continued, however, wolves prowling around behind the herd seemed to unnerve the musk oxen. Gradually the situation changed into one in which the oxen were more scattered, and the wolves walked about between subgroups. Every now and then a skirmish developed when an ox charged a wolf, even though other wolves and musk oxen just stood around nearby.

Such maneuvering and skirmishing interested the wolves more, and soon they became more active. The unevenness of the terrain may also have played a role, for when an ox ran, it had to maintain its footing while carrying its great weight on spindly legs in and out of the troughs without stumbling. Whatever the case, the pace increased, and wolves actually began chasing subgroups of musk oxen. As soon as they got close, the oxen would swing around, stand, and threaten. However, with seven wolves chasing various groups, and the groups trying to keep together, the entire herd began gyrating.

The wolves grew increasingly excited. Soon they started darting in and out among the frantic musk oxen, often passing within inches of them. The shaggy oxen would turn and charge with lowered heads, and strike out with front hoofs. Through our lenses, the scene grew surrealistic: big dark whirling beasts; long white streaks; clouds of dust; swerving, streaking, twisting, charging; black masses, white streaks, dust—the Stone Age!

Fourteen musk oxen and seven wolves, all in a swirling, chaotic, dusty mass. The noise, the dust, the motion, the frenzy, drew us straight into the fray. It grew hard to remain objective. Although I have watched wolf packs chasing moose, deer, and caribou, that was always from an airplane, where I was clearly a spectator. It was different here. We were almost in the middle of this primeval scene, especially since the wolves streaking among those massive oxen were not just wolves. They were Scruffy, Mom, Mid-Back, Alpha Male, Left Shoulder, Shaggy, and the Lone Ranger.

I was certain we would see one of our wolves killed or seriously hurt. The herd was reluctant to run far, so the attack turned into a localized harassment, back and forth on the flats, up and down through the troughs. The wolves clearly handled the terrain better. Once an ox even fell over and lay on its back with all four feet up in the air, and the wolves rushed in and nipped at it.

It's hard to say how long the skirmishing went on. We completely lost track of time, but it probably lasted an hour or more, and the pace kept increasing. Run, stand, run, stand, run, stand. Run, run, stand; run, run, stand; run, run, run, stand; run, run, run, run, run. The herd panicked.

"We're going to see a kill!" Jim shouted prophetically.

Thirty seconds later, Alpha Male and Mom closed in on a calf, and Mom grabbed it by the right side of its head. Alpha Male latched onto its nose. The rest of the pack quickly gravitated to the pair and their quarry, while the calf's mother joined the stampeding herd. As the calf struggled, it gradually dragged the six wolves stuck to its head and shoulders down a slope.

Then, suddenly, Left Shoulder, who had the most posterior grasp on the calf's right side, let up and rushed off after the herd, which, now in a complete rout, was fleeing down off the plateau into the creek bottom. Mid-Back, who had the last hold on the calf's other side, soon left to join him. They hit the second calf crossing the creek.

The herd turned to its right and rushed down the creekbed one hundred yards to a river. One big bull stopped and stood its ground. More wolves left the first calf, while Mom and Alpha Male held their grip. The calf was no longer on its feet, and soon the male left. Down in the creek, Left Shoulder and Mid-Back worked on the second calf, as their packmates joined them. And in the distance, the remaining twelve musk oxen, including a calf, were fleeing up the side of the huge bank toward another plateau. The calf and a couple of adults were far to the rear.

Then—I couldn't believe it—fifty yards behind the musk oxen, far away on the hillside, ran another wolf, either Shaggy or Mid-Back. She was after the third calf! The calf was running along the right side of an adult, and another adult was fifteen feet behind. The wolf caught up quickly, and just at the top of the hill, she grabbed the calf from the right. The adults continued to run, except for the two with the calf. But the closer one did not face the wolf, and the other had stopped partway up the hill. Alpha Male arrived and joined the female wolf. The calf continued to struggle and eventually dragged both wolves all the way back down the hill to the river. There they were joined by others, and the calf fell.

Still the job was not over. The frenzied wolves now became very intent and businesslike. No greetings, no socializing. They reminded me of firefighters springing to life to put out a fire. But the wolves' goal was to remove as much from the kills as they could as quickly as possible. It seemed now like each wolf considered the others competitors. Each would feed for twenty minutes to almost an hour, then sneak off furtively and regurgitate into a cache. Several interspersed this activity with wading into the river and drinking. Mom and Scruffy took loads up to the den right away, and others did later. Alpha Male remained near the kill for hours.

While I sat and watched the wolves at work close up, preparing to convert the recent calves to wolf pups, I realized what an extraordinarily rare observation I had made. It happens all the time in the High Arctic, of course, but there's usually nobody around to watch.

CHAPTER EIGHT

Adaptation

JIM BRANDENBURG

JIM BRANDENBURG *is one of the most acclaimed photographers in North America. His work has appeared in such magazines as* Audubon, Natural History, *and* Life, *but he is perhaps best known as a veteran contract photographer for* National Geographic. *His many awards include the Magazine Photographer of the Year Award, and awards from the World Press Institute, Kodak, the British Broadcasting System, and the National Press Photographers Association. He lives in Minnesota, and describes his assignment to photograph the white wolves of the Canadian Arctic as "the highlight of my career as a wildlife photographer."*

AS A PHOTOGRAPHER, I will confess to a touch of aesthetic vanity. In summer, when the wolves were at the peak of their dishevelment, I could barely contain my urge to approach them with a dog brush and comb out this bumper crop of flotsam. Though they would never have consented to such an indignity, they might have appreciated the gesture. On hot days, the wolves appeared to find their excess hair a bother, and they would often take a favorite spot of dusty sand to roll around on their backs and try to rid themselves of it. All summer, I waited for the moment when all the old excess hair would be gone and the wolves would seem eminently sleek and smooth, but such a day never came.

No sooner had the last vestiges of the old been shed than the coming winter's fur began to appear.

None of this is meant to suggest that the wolves were free from vanity themselves—or at least a primitive sense of hygiene. Most had a definite interest in staying clean and white. One of the most remarkable scenes I have ever witnessed in the animal world involved Buster's fastidiousness in this regard.

During a particularly muddy day in the spring, he scared up an Arctic hare and proceeded to chase it in ever tightening circles. Though out of camera range, I was able to watch him through binoculars. It took him close to ten minutes to catch up with his prey and in the process he had turned almost black with accumulated mud. While I expected him to lie down in panting triumph and eat his meal, he instead held the dead hare firmly in his jaws, trotted with his head held high to the nearest fjord and hopped into the water. For the next few minutes, he swam around until he had washed off all the mud. He climbed out of the water, sleek with brine, the hare still untasted in his mouth. Then he began to shake himself dry in that telltale canine fashion that begins with a vibration of the head and shoulders and culminates with a whiplashing of the tail. Only then, when his coat was restored to immaculate condition, did he begin to eat, like a nobleman who would not think of coming to the table without the proper dinner jacket.

Etiquette probably had little to do with Buster's behavior. In a year-around environment of snow and ice, white fur provides great camouflage. Whether the urge to stay clean is instinctive, learned, or some combination of the two, there were definite variations among the wolves in terms of the premium they put on cleanliness.

Left Shoulder was a particular stickler for cleanliness; his coat was always the whitest of the pack. Scruffy, on the other hand, seemed to have a typically adolescent repugnance for the bath. Perhaps, being a young wolf, he had not yet learned how much easier it was to wash off mud and blood *before* they had had a chance to dry into a kind of Arctic adobe.

Another fascinating aspect of the wolf coat took me a year to figure out: the dark masks that would appear and disappear on their faces. In the case of Lone Ranger, the mask was pretty much a constant, but the others would develop similar masks for weeks on end. At first I speculated that the masks were an odd artifact of the summer pelage, like the temporary dark streaks females like Midback would develop on their backs. It wasn't until I witnessed a musk ox kill that I learned the masks were actually bloodstains mixed with dirt; they occurred after every feeding in which the wolves would thrust their snouts into a fresh-killed carcass. Though I sometimes saw a submissive wolf lick the still-wet blood from the muzzle of an alpha in an ultimate appeasement gesture, more often than not the blood was still viscous when the wolves went to cache the excess meat. To do this, they dug shallow holes in the dirt, deposited the meat, and then used their noses to tamp a layer of soil on top of it. Given the exigencies of such feeding practices, the masks were inevitable.

The legendary olfactory acuity of wolves is another example of their superb adaptation to their environment. It has been reported in the scientific literature that the surface area receptive to smells in the nose of a wolf is 14 times larger than that of a human. Some scientists estimate that wolves can smell a hundred times better than we can. Humans are like the blind in comparison. Between poppy blossoms and offal, there is an extraordinarily rich and detailed world of smells that is beyond our abilities to detect. For wolves, though, a breeze provides a constant stream of information about their world.

As with many predators that rely on wind-borne scents to help them find prey, the Arctic wolves tested the wind constantly; their snouts are always cocked in the direction of the prevailing breezes. They seemed particularly agitated and disgruntled on excessively windy days, no doubt finding the flood of random information at once tantalizing and annoying. On these days, they would avoid hunting altogether and wait for a day of steady and moderate information flow.

On one ideal, low breeze day, I followed the pack members on a hunting expedition. They were loping along in their typically indefatigable fashion, testing the breeze occasionally as they proceeded upwind. Suddenly, Midback began to act very excited and focused, and her mood was quickly picked up by her fellow hunters. I could neither see nor smell any reason for this exuberance, but I raced ahead, skirting a small rise in the direction they were headed. There, off in the distance, was a musk ox herd.

On another occasion, I followed several of the wolves to a nearby beach, where they located a dead fish washed up on the shore. The fish, an Arctic char, had been dead for some time; it smelled quite rank. The wolves, who were usually so fastidious with their white coats, lay down on the fish and began rolling around on it until they had all become steeped in the stench. It seemed bizarre. When they took off on a hunt shortly thereafter, it began to make sense. They were evidently masking their own scent with something their prey had no fear of. While I did not join them on this outing, I wondered if the stratagem proved successful. No need to worry, a hapless musk ox might have reassured itself on some primal level of consciousness: *It's only a dead fish stalking me.*

The wolves' eyesight and hearing were in many regards as impressive as their sense of smell. Once I noticed Buster looking very intently at something across the valley from the den. Because he was staring downwind, I knew it was not smell that had attracted his attention. Try as I might, though, I was unable to glimpse anything unusual. Then I got my binoculars and began carefully scanning the area Buster found so fascinating. After a few minutes of searching, I finally saw an Arctic hare so far away it barely looked like a dot to me without the binoculars' magnification.

To test the wolves' hearing range, Mech and I once tried a little experiment. After synchronizing our watches, he headed off to the distant hinterlands while I remained near the den. At a prearranged time, Mech howled. He was much too far away for me to hear, but the wolves appeared to have no trouble whatsoever. They cocked their ears in curiosity, then tilted their heads back and emitted a chorus of replies.

Excellence in all these sensory departments allows the wolves to do more than just locate prey efficiently. Wolves probably are one of the most social animals outside of the primates, and the success of the pack depends strongly on a highly developed system of communication, not only within a pack but between neighboring packs as well. Smell, vision and hearing play crucial roles in such communication.

Consider, for example, the role of scent-marking. Whenever the pack was out roaming around, they would stop every so often to urinate on prominent marker spots, the fire hydrants of the Arctic. Boulders, their favorite iceberg and other prominent spots like our *inukshuks* and tents were regular targets.

They were not doing this to relieve their bladders. In typical canine fashion, they were so adept at rationing small squirts of urine that it seemed they would never run dry. There was one spot in particular, about 15 miles from the den, that they would greet with exceptional tail-wagging excitement. Every time they came to this spot, each wolf would sniff happily and appear to scrutinize the reams of messages they and their fellows had left over the decades. Then they would urinate and defecate once again, adding yet another chapter to the olfactory history of their clan.

Theories abound as to why wolves indulge in scent-marking. Some scientists suggest that the wolves are actually setting out a mapping system to help them pinpoint their exact location within their territory. Their evident excitement at discovering a traditional marking spot tends to reinforce this theory. When I watched them come upon such a spot, they seemed almost to emit a great collective sigh of relief—home again.

It is likely that the wolves are, via the mapping process, simultaneously erecting a boundary to tell adjacent packs to stay out. One evidence for this is the fact that wolves leave their "calling cards" with much greater frequency on the perimeter of their territory rather than in the interior. I am virtually certain that individual wolves can distinguish the urine of their packmates from that of strangers. As with human tribes, clearly defined boundaries reduce internecine fighting; good fences, even olfactory ones, do make good neighbors. Wolves, ill-suited to the art of construction, build instead a kind of Urine Curtain; the more pack members there are to participate, the stronger the wall and the greater the deterrence against invaders.

The sonic equivalent of scent-marking is the wolf's howl. Often I watched the whole pack, including the pups, join ranks in a great collective songfest. Each had his or her distinctive voice and a preferred range of notes. Midback, for instance, had a high-pitched, almost whiny cry that stood out in comic contrast to human stereotypes. Left Shoulder, on the other hand, would howl in the lower octaves. One thing was certain. Whatever their preferred notes, wolves seem to hate hitting the same note as a packmate, and when this happened by accident, they frantically shuffled about until discord was once more reestablished.

This is a fascinating behavior that I had previously witnessed in Minnesota with a pack of five captive timber wolf puppies that I had occasion to raise near my home. "The boys," as I referred to them, had accepted me as a surrogate packmate. Many evenings, I'd howl back and forth with them, apparently to our mutual delight. Whenever I would try to match a note that one of them was hitting, however, he would immediately change pitch. This was but one of many captive timber wolf behaviors that correlated almost exactly with behaviors observed in the wild Arctic pack.

The reason for the wolves' contempt for harmony is well-rooted in evolution. Studies have shown that their predilection for cacophony is highly pragmatic. By varying their tones, a pack can project the impression of greater size; adjacent packs presumably will think twice before engaging in territorial encroachment, dissuaded by the rank on rank of phantoms echoing in the night. I know I have been fooled. Once, while winter camping in Minnesota, I heard a wild pack howling in the distance and estimated the size to be at least eight wolves. Later, however, while snowshoeing across a cedar bog, I came across the pack feeding on a previously killed moose. The entire pack consisted of only four wolves.

Howling begins at a very early age as an offshoot of the yips and food-begging whines that pups offer whenever they are hungry, that is to say, at practically every waking moment. Within weeks of their emergence from the den, the pups cock their tiny snouts to the sky right alongside their parents.

Wolves howl for many reasons beyond signaling their location to other packs. When several pack members are left behind at the den while the others go off on a hunt, both groups will sometimes howl back and forth; the former perhaps out of hunger and disgruntlement, the latter perhaps to communicate their position and keep in touch with the home base.

After a long sleep, too, wolves will howl, perhaps to work up group enthusiasm for the next hunt. In this regard, they reminded me of team athletes shouting in unison before a big game. Often on Ellesmere I watched this lupine *reveille,* and the ritual seldom varied. One wolf, usually the alpha female, would wake up first, yawn, stretch a few times, and walk around sniffing her packmates. Then she would begin to howl, as if to say, *Hey guys, it's time to go hunting.* One by one, the others would rise up and start howling, the pups included, and soon their voices would echo through the surrounding valleys.

Beautiful as this chorus was to me, to any prey within earshot it must have been a worrisome sound. Perhaps this was yet another reason for howling—an attempt to add one more enervating stress to the lives of those they wished to catch. Sinister overtones aside, sometimes wolves seem to howl purely for pleasure. It's impossible to watch them singing, in their animation and amiability toward one another, and not get some sense that they are enjoying themselves.

At times like this, the urge to start howling with

them can be overwhelming. In northern Minnesota, I had done this many times at night, not only with the pups I raised but also with wild packs living near my home. It is hard to describe the satisfaction that comes from such "discourse." When Mech and I got to Ellesmere, though, we resolved to steadfastly avoid giving in to this impulse near the den site for fear it would upset the pack.

For most of the summer, we kept to this agreement. Late in the season, however, with Mech back in the United States, I found myself one sunlit night listening to a magnificent song session. At this point, I had been living alone with the pack for a couple of weeks, and the absence of human communication might have influenced me. In any event, the temptation to join in and howl overcame me. I just couldn't contain myself. My head snapped back, my lips pursed, and I raised cupped hands to my mouth in makeshift simulation of a resonant snout—*Aaaah ooooooo! Aaah aah aah ooooooooooo!*

I had barely enjoyed a single moment of trans-species satisfaction when Buster and his cohorts cut short their own howls and began acting in an unusually agitated way. Surveying me with eyes more piercing than I had ever seen in them, the alpha animals became especially "hyper" and suspicious. Buster immediately took charge of the investigation. His ears stiffened, his tail became erect, and he started to prance nervously as he approached me.

Perhaps he and the others assumed that another pack was lurking right behind me. Or maybe they thought I had metamorphosed into a strange, deformed wolf of bipedal design. That they became so upset should not have surprised me. If one of them had started to blather away in English gibberish, I would have been upset, too! They remained agitated for much of the next week before they settled down. I, of course, did not repeat the experiment. For whatever reason, the wolves preferred to think of me as anything but another wolf.

CHAPTER NINE

The Master Hunters

WILLIAM O. PRUITT, JR.

WILLIAM O. PRUITT, JR., *was born in 1922. He has
studied the ecology of arctic animals in northern Canada,
Alaska, Finland, Sweden, and the former Soviet Union.
His Taiga Biological Station has become a recognized center
for teaching and research on winter ecology. His writing
has appeared in such magazines as* Harper's *and*
Scientific American, *and has been described as "a rare
marriage of sound ecology and superb prose." He is also the
author of two books,* Wild Harmony *(1960) and a short
textbook entitled* Boreal Ecology *(1978). Dr. Pruitt is
the recipient of an honorary degree from the University of
Alaska and is a member of the Ernest Thompson Seton
Foundation, Inc., Board of Advisors. He is currently a
professor of zoology at the University of Manitoba.*

IN THE PALE BLUE BOWL of the sky the sun traveled
on an annular path around the zenith. For a week the
sun had not dropped below the horizon and it would
not be out of sight for yet another week. The land on
which it shone was north of the Arctic Circle—a treeless, rolling land of long parallel ridges and swales. In
late June there was still ice on the lakes, and many of
the swales and ravines were full of snow. This snow was
not the hard wind-carved snow of the tundra winter but
remnants of it—a heavy, wet, crystalline stuff that collapsed underfoot.

As the sun's heat reflected from the earth in shim-
mering waves the variegated pattern of heat-absorbing

gravel ridge and heat-reflecting snow bank caused weird mirages. The distant hills floated above the horizon as battlements and crenelated towers, then sank out of sight only to rise again in a new form.

On the crest of a gravel ridge a wolf appeared. Her coat of steel-gray was ragged and worn, with great tufts of the long winter hairs hanging loose. In her jaws she carried the lifeless body of a ground squirrel. As she trotted over the ridge the squirrel's tail flopped loosely, as did the tufts of long winter fur remaining on her lean flanks. The female was emaciated from the metabolic drain of lactation. The ground squirrel's carcass was lean, too, but every bit of meat helped to fill her pups and to lessen their urgent nuzzlings for her milk.

Far ahead of the wolf the pattern of parallel ridge and swale was broken by a higher ridge which traced a sinuous course toward the wavering horizon. This ridge was not gravel but was composed of sand, with steep sides and with smears of twisted dwarf birch and willow in protected niches. Such a ridge is an esker, a legacy of the not so distant days when the great continental ice sheet had scoured the land. The ice sheet had finally stagnated and begun to waste away. Meltwater had poured through a monstrous crevasse in the ice and finally choked the crevasse with churned-up sand. The sinuous deposit of sand, miles long, had become the esker and, because of the easy digging, it provided a den site for the wolf and her mate.

The den had been originally excavated by Arctic foxes but wolves, many generations ago, had preempted it. Each breeding season, they had enlarged and modified the original den until now it was a labyrinth of narrow tunnels and entrances. Only a small portion was used each year by the adult wolves but the pups had free range through all the tunnels.

The gray female wolf trotted over the last gravel ridge and abruptly changed her course. She circled far around the den until she was downwind of it and then approached upwind. As she came up to it she gave voice to a throaty, chuckling noise. A chorus of puppy yelps and squeals answered and a mass of fur boiled out of the den entrance. The fur separated into five pups who cavorted toward the female and swarmed around her, tugging at the squirrel in her mouth. She released the squirrel and it was claimed by two of the pups who started worrying the carcass. The remaining pups nuzzled the female's mouth and head, licking and chewing her thick throat fur. She extended her neck and lowered her head. Her sides heaved and she regurgitated the remains of three more ground squirrels.

It had been a successful hunt—the lucky find of a shallow, easily excavated ground squirrel burrow that had yielded not only the young squirrels but an adult as well. Not often did the wolf have this kind of luck. Sometimes she returned to the den empty-mouthed, empty-stomached, or with only a portion of a long-dead caribou fawn carcass. Her mate hunted assiduously, also. He usually cached his contributions some distance from the den—too far for the pups to find it. The female used these caches for her own food.

Her mate had now been absent for two days. The female felt uneasy and restless, for the pups were big enough to try to follow her away from the den and only the most forceful nips sent them yelping back to it. Even so, they usually saw her returning and met her nearly a quarter mile from the den. Her motivation to return to the den site was waning while her restlessness was the waxing of the next phase of the yearly cycle— the urge to travel and hunt with a group, her pups and her mate.

Now the pups had consumed the squirrels, and the combination of full bellies and hot sun took effect. They sprawled out in attitudes which had one thing in common—complete relaxation. The warm sun caused drowsiness in the female and her head dropped lower. Finally she, too, rolled over onto her side and let the sun's heat flow through her.

The pups slept soundly but the female frequently roused, lifted her head for a look around the horizon, and collapsed again. During one such look her eye caught a flash of white on a distant ridge. Instantly she sat up and focused on it. Was it the big white wolf that was her mate, or was it caribou? Caribou does at this time of the year have bleached, worn pelage and from a distance would appear as white animals.

No, the outline and movements were not of caribou but were wolflike. The female rose, stretched, and eased her way around the group of sleeping pups. Once clear of the den site she broke into a trot and went toward the food-cache where the wolf pair usually met.

As the big white male came nearer she could see he was bedraggled and limped slightly. Actually he had nearly lost his life the day before when, swimming a swollen river, he had been rammed by a big block of floating ice and squeezed between it and the river bank. Only a fortunate turn of the ice block and some frantic struggles on his part had enabled him to scramble free. As it was, he had lain immobile for nearly a day until the pain in his leg and side had subsided.

When he approached, his tail went up. The female, seeing this, lowered her head and danced sideways toward him. Then she rolled on her back before him and placed both forepaws onto his shoulders in the traditional greeting ceremony of paired wolves. The two wolves return to the den site, where the white male collapsed, stretched, and slept. Nose on paws, the female lay on the mound above the den and watched.

As the pups grew older the family group became more effective as a hunting unit. Soon the pups were weaned, and without the drain of lactation the female put on weight and her fur became sleek.

Food became plentiful during the tundra summer. Many creatures migrated to the tundra to raise their young. The annual population maximum coincided with the wolves' need for extra food. Lemmings, voles, Arctic hares, caribou—all reached their yearly peak in numbers. The inexorable laws of population mathematics have decreed that all this great surplus must be sacrificed before the next breeding season, all except parental replacements. Thus, lemmings, voles, Arctic hares, and caribou accept the sacrifice of surplus vegetation; Arctic foxes, weasels, and wolves accept the sacrifice of surplus lemmings, voles, Arctic hares, and caribou; while the inescapable bacteria and organisms of decay accept the sacrifice of all and make the circle complete.

This intricate interweaving of relationships that results in the tundra ecosystem is clearly a fragile thing. The annual energy input is quite low. It is parceled among comparatively few species, in contrast to a tropical rain forest, for example. Thus, perturbations within one species population have a far greater effect than would be the case in the tropical forest. Likewise, injury to the system is corrected or healed slowly. Many tundra animals have evolved mechanisms which prevent permanent damage to the ecosystem. The populations of lemmings and voles "crash" regularly, thus preventing overgrazing and permanent damage to their range.

Caribou meet the problem in a different way—they migrate. When the first storms of winter begin to rework and harden the snow cover of the tundra, the caribou migrate to regions of softer snow. As the wolves stay where they can contact caribou, they too perform a geographic migration to the taiga along with the caribou.

For creatures accustomed to the eye-stretching freedom of the tundra, the northern coniferous forest, or taiga, presented a fearsome situation. The trees towered over the pups, seeming to press upon them, and restricting their field of vision. A whole new world of scents assailed them—spruce gum and birch sap, red squirrel, spruce grouse, and moose. And moose! Here was a fearsome creature indeed.

The first encounter one of the pups had with a moose nearly proved his undoing. On an independent exploring trip along a game trail through a frozen muskeg, he crossed a strange scent-drift. He turned and followed it at a run. Suddenly a huge bull moose confronted him with an expanse of palmate antlers, great splayed hoofs, and guttural snorts. The pup made a flying leap to avoid the bull's charge. He had no chance to recover his composure because the bull made a turf-tearing swing and charged again. The pup fled. Only a very skilled or very hungry wolf would face those murderous hoofs without the aid of deep or crusted snow to hinder the movements of such a formidable creature.

Winter closed in. The wolf family group found that hunting food in the sub-Arctic taiga was more difficult than it had been on the Arctic prairies. True, the forest afforded stalking cover, but it also had thick soft snow. Although the caribou travel with ease through snow deep enough to flounder a wolf, they felt constant alarm in the forest. Thus both species reverted as much as they could to something that resembled their ancestral habitat. The caribou rested on open, windswept lakes where the footing and visibility were good. Because the wolves were cursorial beasts, whenever possible they traveled on the lakes, where they, too, had good footing and visibility.

The wolf family, white male leading, trotted single file through the snow onto the lake. As they padded over the wind-hardened snow they came into the view of a band of caribou that were resting on the lake. The caribou, all alert with ear funnels tipped and nostrils wide, stood and faced the wolves. The wolf silhouettes slowly changed shape as the wolves moved across the lake. The caribou relaxed. Several lay down again and resumed the never-ending chore of ruminants—chewing their cud. No stimulus of danger had been received; digestion could proceed. The wolf silhouettes disappeared into the forest beyond the lake.

For a week the wolf family had used a dense spruce stand as a base of operations. Here they had packed the snow down hard and made trails to all the neighboring lakes. The wolves had scratched and melted sleeping holes in the snow under the thickest spruce clumps.

One pup awoke. He rose, stretched, and yawned luxuriously. In size he and his sibs were hardly pups. In fact, he was already larger than most sled dogs and his feet were twice the size of a dog's. But in hunting ability, and especially in his knowledge of the intricacies and niceties of wolf social behavior, he was still very much a callow adolescent.

The pup sidled to the big white male and lay down in front of him. The white male opened one eye and rumbled in his throat. The pup thumped his tail. He had learned enough to know this was merely a sleepy greeting. A slightly different tone and timbre would be present in an actual warning. The pup reached out a paw and gently caught the claws in the male's neck-ruff. The male opened his jaws and caught the pup's leg, and his rumbles increased in volume. In ecstasy at this attention, the pup then rolled onto his back, extended his other forepaw and snagged the opposite side of the male's neck-ruff. Without rising, the big male slid closer and transferred his jaw grip from the pup's leg to his neck-ruff. He shook it gently, making fierce rumblings in his throat. The pup suddenly squealed— his neck-ruff was not as thick and protecting as an adult's. The male immediately relaxed his grip, stood, shook himself thoroughly, and stretched. Putting up his nose, he partly opened his mouth and howled softly. Instantly all the pups and the steel-gray female were on their feet. After a confusion of shaking, stretching, nose-touching, and tail-wagging, one by one they gave tentative howls and then all joined chorus.

"Howling" is a poor word to use. "Singing" would be better, except that we have anthropocentric connotations attached to the word. In our language, a male bluebird in his belligerent defense of territory is said to "sing," whereas a wolf in expressing a feeling of well-being can only be said to "howl."

After the singing ceremony the white male leaped completely over the nearest pup and pranced away along the packed trail. All followed. One of the pups turned aside to snuffle at a mouse ventilator shaft in the snow. The female nipped his heel, causing him to leap back onto the trail. They were on more serious business now and after larger game than mice.

As they topped the ridge they could see below them the white expanse of a large snow-covered lake where several bands of caribou were resting. All the bands were far out on the lake, where the snow was wind-worked and hard; none was near the shore where the snow, protected from wind, lay thick and soft.

The big white male began his stalk. A wolf "stalk" is actually a straightforward sort of thing, not creeping or crawling but simply a slow, steady walk forward. Creeping and bellying are for ambushers such as the lynx; the wolf is a chaser, a runner.

Out onto the lake went the group, plowing through the soft edge-snow. A caribou doe threw up her head and aimed her stimulus-gathering apparatus—eyes, ear funnels, nostrils. The silhouette she received focused across a threshold of stimulation and she threw out one hind leg sideways. Her awkward stance was noted immediately by the remainder of the band and they all turned their sensory windows in the direction she indicated.

The wolves continued their steady advance. The first doe, who clearly had a lower reaction threshold than the others of the band, rose onto her hind legs, turned, and bounded away, then settled into a swinging trot. The remainder of the band exploded after her leaving a trail of flying snow and breath-steam. At the first wheel of the fleeing caribou the wolves broke into a run. The big white male soon slackened his pace, but the pups jostled around him. Long ago he had learned that when caribou fled like that—in a tight group without stragglers—no wolf could overtake them. The pups would have to learn this basic truth for themselves. He resumed his steady trot and was rejoined by the female.

The two adult wolves had crossed the lake and were well up the next ridge before the pups returned, panting and steaming, tongues flapping. As the excess heat flowed away from them, the temperature of their fur slowly dropped again—the frost-line closing in. Each was suddenly clothed in white as the frost-line reached the tips of the long guard hairs and the body-steam crystallized onto them.

The two adult wolves trotted onward, constantly

reading the air for the scent of caribou. Each ridge had to be approached and topped in its own way, depending on the flow of air currents. Each caribou trail had to be snuffled and tested for freshness of scent.

Here was real appetitive behavior—a searching, a craving that could be fulfilled only by the consummatory act. For the adult wolves the appetitive stimulus was particularly strong since it was reinforced by the sight and sound of their hungry pups.

The sun was sliding along the southern horizon by the time the wolves came down to another lake. No caribou were on it, because they had already completed their rest and rumination cycle and had returned to the forest to continue their ceaseless search for food. Their scent was still strong in the bowl-shaped resting spots in the snow, and the pellets of excreta were yet unfrozen. The scent of caribou was so strong that one of the pups gave a small squeak of excitement.

The adult wolves broke into a lope and flowed through the fringe of willows at the lake's edge. Ahead, they could see caribou. Again there was the startled focusing of eyes and ears. No need for the alarm pose now, only the upward thrust with the hind legs, the turning and fleeing. One big buck wavered before taking a choice of escape routes. His fleeting moment of hesitation slowed the wheel of fortune and the ball of natural selection dropped into his slot. That moment of hesitation, the difference between immediate response to a stimulus and a slightly delayed response, was all that was needed to release the wolves' chase, the consummatory act.

The chase was swift and violent. Caribou and wolves crashed through a willow thicket. The big white male pulled alongside and leaped. He hit the caribou on the shoulder. The great jaws closed on the neck. They twisted. The female and pups hit at the same time. Caribou and wolves went down in a cloud of snow, fur, flailing hoofs, and flashing teeth. The hot smell of blood flowed as a cloud of steam billowed. The caribou kicked feebly and was still. Natural selection has been served.

In the voluminous folklore about wolves there is a recurring theme: "A wolf can catch any animal it chases." We can now understand how this belief has arisen. The wolf can indeed catch any animal it chases; it doesn't really chase any beast unless the chances of success are very high. The probability of success is established very soon after contact—the limp, the slow turn, the delayed escape-reaction; these are the "releasers" that trigger the change from the flexible, searching, appetitive behavior phase to the stereotyped, deadly efficient consummatory phase. If the proper stimuli are not displayed the consummatory act is not released and the searching, appetitive behavior continues. The wolves must exhibit or present their "danger-stimulus" complex many times before an appropriate releasing response is obtained. Once it is obtained, success is virtually assured.

When one understands the behavioral sequences leading to a successful hunt, then the biological role of the wolf as a terminal carnivore becomes clearer. The culling function is seen.

Data are available to support this concept. A comparison of two widely separated caribou populations, one "protected" for many years by bounties, poison, and aircraft hunting of wolves, and the other population "protected" for only one year, revealed that the percentage of limping or obviously sick caribou in the more "protected" population was about twice the percentage in the less "protected" population. The genetic and evolutionary implications are obvious. This is the raw material for natural selection.

While crossing a frozen lake one day in midwinter, the wolves' attention was attracted by the sight of black objects against the white snow. They changed course to investigate. As they drew closer they distinguished two small spruce trees protruding above the snow. For any canine, such a thing must be investigated closely.

The scent of caribou hit their nostrils. The adult wolves slid to a stop—caribou scent without any other sign? The incomplete pattern of stimuli caused the big white male to rumble warningly. Three of the pups turned back and rejoined the adults, but the other two dashed on toward the trees. Between the trees they encountered the source of the scent—the hind half of a caribou, buried in the snow. Their hunger and inexperience caused them to forget the formalities of group feeding, and they began tearing and gnawing at the frozen meat.

The adults and other pups circled slowly around the trees, searching the snow for scent. A faint, strange, oily odor caused the big male's hackles to rise, his throaty rumbling changed tone. Another strange scent, faint yet acrid, hit his nostrils. His tail stiffened, his ears went back, and he leaped sideways, then turned and streaked across the snow. The others followed. All except the two pups eating at the carcass. They looked up at the sudden movement, then both gave convulsive grunts as their intercostal muscles hardened in strychnine tetany. They fell stiffly onto their sides. Blood spurted from their severed tongues as their contracting jaw muscles forced their teeth through the flesh. Bodies deprived of oxygen, their eyes bulged. After a few minutes the muscles relaxed and one pup drew a few shallow breaths. Partially revived, he struggled to a half-sitting position. Suddenly his tail threshed wildly, his spine arched as muscles contracted and hardened again. His toes flexed sharply. Suffocation squeezed his life away.

Long after the two wolves died, ravens circled down to the exposed caribou meat. After feeding, they, too, died lingering deaths. One raven staggered into the air and flew half a mile over the forest before fluttering down through the trees. A fox found the raven carcass, devoured it, and died, convulsing, in the snow. A wolverine loped over the lake surface, ate of the poisoned caribou, and jerked through the snow into the forest. The wolverine's amazing resistance to strychnine enabled him to travel for two miles, struggling and snapping at the fire in his stomach, before he too died. From the poison station, pain, death, and destruction spread out over the land like ripples on a pond.

In primeval times the wolf was found all over North America—in the deciduous forests of the eastern seaboard, with the bison herds on the central grasslands, in the mountains and intermontane deserts of the Southwest, in the sub-Arctic taiga and Arctic tundra. The native peoples of North America recognized the wolf as their competitor and the master hunter, and respected him for it. More important, they recognized and cherished the interdependence of all living things. Indeed, the Alaskan Eskimo expressed it as a proverb, "Innuit neli-kranya," meaning roughly "Fish eat fish, weasel eat mice, all the same as man." Only recently has such a concept of the eco-logical community entered the white man's thoughts.

North America was invaded by white men who believed not in the pantheistic philosophy of the interwoven ecological com-munity, but in the Judaic-Christian idea of "dominion over the beasts of the field." This invasion presaged the doom of many organisms and systems—the sea mink, the eastern de-ciduous forests, the woodland bison, the plains bison, the wind-resisting prairie sod, the California grizzly, the passen-ger pigeon. With this invasion the wolf's range began to shrink. At first the destruction of his food supply was more effective than the active efforts against him. The wolf's last stand in the western United States brought forth white man's supreme weapon—poison. Against it no species can survive.

In former days, when intensive food production was vital to our country's economy, the use of poison to protect pioneer cattle herds was perhaps justified. But today, with our ever-growing surpluses of meat and meat products, such efforts to implement meat production only compound a national illness. The more recent adoption of the use of poison in "wildlife man-agement" only reflects the widespread ignorance of biological principles.

Today the master hunter, with the hand of man still against him, is restricted mainly to the North—the tundra and the taiga.

In the taiga the day lengthens, the sun swings higher in the sky, the winter grows stale. The snow, once soft and fluffy, becomes crystalline and crusted. The caribou become restless as it hinders their movements. One day the threshold of sensitivity is reached. A certain level of hardness and density of the snow releases the constrained urge to move, to walk, to follow another's tracks. All through the taiga, caribou begin to move away from the advancing spring. The migration is on.

Within the wolves the gonads ripen. The howling ceremonies take on a new meaning, and a new sound. Now the howling is truly singing. The big white male once again courts the steel-gray female. Their first spring, the pups are full grown but not sexually mature. Family ties are still strong and will remain so until next spring, when the pups will be old enough to strike out alone.

A restlessness afflicts the wolves, too. They become aware of the sharp ablation needles on the snow surface. The caribou trails stretch before them, broad, hard, and inviting. The wolves move along them. The steel-gray female leads, for she has a strong urge to revisit a land of long parallel ridges and swales, a land where the mirages float above the horizon, where the great sand esker twists across the landscape.

CHAPTER TEN
Wolf Woods
ROGER PETERS

ROGER PETERS *is a graduate of the University of Chicago and the University of Michigan. He received his doctorate at the latter institution for his studies on the learning abilities of wolves. He is currently a professor of psychology at Fort Lewis College in Colorado.*

YELLOW AND LIME LEAFLETS played peekaboo in sunlit tree-tops, Labrador tea flourished in the receding snow, and even the lichen seemed alive. On north-facing slopes, though, the snow was still knee-deep; old-timers claimed they could find enough to make ice cream on the Fourth of July.

The morning was cold enough to make me sprint back to the lodge after dumping each load in my trunk, cold enough, I hoped, to keep the wolf recta frozen until I got to Northton, where I would pack them in dry ice before I joined Hunt at the meetings. I stowed them in the corner, where they would do the least damage if they thawed, then zoomed at Hunt-like speeds to Joe's for a farewell romp with the wolves.

As I strode to the fence, Red and Lotte arched and leaped, gamboling so frantically that even Gray had to dance a little, if only to keep out of their way. I made my escape after only the briefest of romps, backing through the gate like a mandarin, pushing them back as they tried to squeeze past.

I howled from the top of the hill. They replied immediately, Lotte barking and yipping, Red croaking like a raven, and only Gray sounding like a wolf. At Upsala Lake I stopped for a howl to Freya, who did not reply.

I made it to Northton in record time. I met Hunt at the University of Northland, where the AIBS [American Institute of Biological Sciences] meetings were already in progress. My talk went well, in spite of my nervousness. Afterward I went home with Hunt for dinner.

Over dinner Hunt, his family, and I discussed such a variety of topics that wolves were conspicuous by their absence. At its closest approach to that topic the conversation was curiously becalmed. We were discussing Breezy, the dog, a small terrierlike creature of the sort that is ordinarily found in orbit about one's feet, preparing to muffle its yips with a mouthful of ankle. Unlike others of his ilk, however, Breezy, perhaps because of his advancing age, was calm, almost reserved. In an inept attempt to compliment the Hunts on their dog's disposition, I remarked that his size and personality must make him much easier to live with than Hurricane, their wolf, had been.

Hunt and Charlotte exchanged glances. Even the children fell momentarily silent. Suddenly there were dishes to clear, homework assignments to be done, a bed to be made. When we all had retired, I pulled from my pack my well-thumbed copy of Hunt's book and reread the apology with which he had ended his epilogue. I fell asleep with the book on my chest, wondering where Hurricane [a hand-raised wolf pup that had to be placed in a zoo] was now.

I rose with the Hunt family, said a quick farewell, and left for Chicago. By late afternoon, I was on the Kennedy Expressway, threading my way through impending gridlock on my way to an appointment with Daniel Baer at the Chicago Zoo. Baer is a dour, contained man with a wit like water in the desert: seldom near the surface and quicksand when it is. He asked me to describe what kinds of data I hoped to gather at Wolf Woods, as the zoo's wolf exhibit was called. I replied that I was after any variable that might relate to frequency of scent marking, including season, sex, rank, and mood. In his slow, flat basso he pointed out that seasonal data would require observations over a period of at least a year. How often, he asked, did I plan to come to the zoo?

I'd have to see, I answered, but I thought once a month would probably be enough. He suggested that dawn, dusk, and feeding time would be the best times to observe since all activities, including scent marking, are more frequent at those times. Observations at dawn and dusk, when the zoo was closed to the public, would require a key. He rose, led me downstairs to the security office, and issued me one. As I left, I had to force myself not to skip and giggle, for I clutched warmly in my hand a fantasy entertained since my first visit to the Chicago Zoo at the age of eight: a master key to the zoo.

I used my key at dawn and walked unchallenged

through the deserted zoo to Wolf Woods. If Lotte and Red had performed a pas de deux, the Chicago Zoo wolves were the Bolshoi, complete with prima ballerinas, a corps de ballet, and even an audience. A pure white wolf stood atop a large, bare mound, surveying the antics of six others cavorting around it. By the time I reached the fence, I'd seen more hip slams, hackle raisings, snarls, and chases than I would in an entire day at our enclosure in the north. So far I'd seen only seven of the nine wolves, but used as I was to watching only three, they were a horde, a milling mass of indistinguishable animals. How would I ever learn to tell them apart? Learning to identify individuals is the first task of any ethologist conducting a long-term study of a group. In the confusion of that first morning that task seemed impossible.

I had just begun a list of features that I hoped would help me recognize some of the wolves when a diminutive woman with close-cropped ashen hair rode up in an electric golf cart. Her dark-haired female driver produced a stenographic notebook and scribbled frantically as the passenger began calling out pairs of numbers linked by prepositions: "Female Four to Two; Two to Four. Female Six over Male Five. Male Seven to Female Four. Male Seven down." I tried to connect the code to the behavior of the wolves but could not; it was all going much too fast. "Keeper in," said the small woman. That I could understand. A young woman with a heavy bucket had just entered. The wolves formed a line on the mound with military precision. The keeper threw one piece of meat after another, and as each piece sailed through the air, a wolf ran to catch it. Only twice did two lunge simultaneously; each time the woman dictated another pair of numbers. Each wolf took its piece of meat and ran off to consume it away from the others.

Seeing my notebook, the driver asked if I was Peters. Without waiting for a reply, she introduced her companion as Lisa Baer, wife of Daniel. For the next half hour Lisa ran through a crash course in identifying the wolves, gave me a brief history of the pack, and then zoomed off to check her ground squirrel traps, explaining, even as the cart began to move, that she was tagging them in order to map their territories.

In the course of my four-day visit to the zoo I learned that I had just seen Lisa Baer at her slowest speed. Ordinarily she was a blur, appearing at the zoo library, which she was reorganizing; the bookstore, which she managed; the zoo hospital, where she assisted; and, of course, at Wolf Woods, where, with or without her colleague, she gathered more data in twenty minutes than I could manage to get down in an entire day.

Her assistance was invaluable in my continuing attempts to identify the wolves. She pointed out Male Five's dark mask and Male Six's crooked tail, the dark hip patch and rough mane that distinguished Female Seven from Female Eight. She was also able to explain why my counts of the wolves kept coming up short: One wolf, Male Two, rarely left the den.

Male Two, Lisa explained, was the patriarch. Even in captivity wolves are very old at ten. Male Two was sixteen. Crippled by arthritis, he left the den only on the warmest of afternoons, ordinarily remaining inside at mealtime, when another wolf would bring him food. "Watch Female Seven," Lisa advised. "She's been feeding him lately." Sure enough, the next day Female Seven disappeared into the den with a hunk of meat and emerged a few seconds later without it. That afternoon was clear and warm. With temperatures in the fifties, Male Two made an appearance. He was immediately mobbed by the rest of the wolves. They leaped over each other as they tried to lick his face. The melee quickly became a group ceremony that climaxed in a howl. Male Two stood quietly amid the chaos. When the howl subsided, he painfully crept back into the den.

Lisa and Daniel Baer were, like Hunt, victims of the economics of data reduction. Lisa gathered data at feeding time nearly every day, and Daniel spent two weeks during every breeding season taking notes whenever there was enough light to see. Confronted with a choice between gathering new data and analyzing the data they already had, they generally chose the former, for analysis could always be postponed, while the new developments in the relations among the wolves could not. The result was a closetful of notes, only the most interesting ten percent of which ever saw the light of day.

I owed the Baers far more than the data I collected: dawn walks through the deserted zoo; exotic birds shrieking brightly against the low roar of distant traffic; a distant siren and an answering howl. Every morning, as they frolicked in the cold morning air, the wolves revealed new complexities in their dance. I began to realize that any wolf's change of position, posture, or expression affected every other wolf in the enclosure. When Female Six moved to follow a patch of warm sunlight that crept across the rear of the pen, Female Four, the matriarch, watching from her commanding position atop the mound, shifted her position so that Female Six remained under her gaze. Female Five, ambling toward the pond, veered sharply to avoid that gaze, her detour taking her past Male Six, who backed up to avoid her, colliding with Male Seven, who snarled defensively. His snarl drew a low growl from Female Four, as a result of which two other wolves on the mound got up and moved away, displacing Female Six from her patch of sunlight.

The German ethologist Schenkel wrote that every relationship in a pack concerns every member. At Wolf Woods it was easy to see his point. The mechanics of movement were not Newtonian, but they were orderly nonetheless, a calculus of attraction and repulsion, coalition and autonomy, which united the pack in a web of resonating sensitivities.

Half an hour before feeding time on my fourth and last day a young female trotted over to another young wolf and touched his nose with hers. Receiving no response, she raised a forepaw and gently batted at the lying wolf, who rolled over, gaping. The female grabbed his snout. The two jaw-wrestled for a few seconds until the second wolf leaped to his feet and with a bouncy, rocking gait ran behind the mound, the young female snapping at his heels. As soon as she disappeared behind the mound, there was a cartoonlike explosion of barks and yips, and not two but five wolves flew over the top of the mound to stand, panting, by the pond. Female Four trotted around the mound; the young wolves ran to greet her. They crowded around, each using hip slams and sinuous wriggles to interpose itself between Female Four and the others. Female Four stood regally, with head and tail high, suffering their enthusiasm with great dignity. The older wolves, scattered in various shady nooks about the enclosure, now began to appear, stretching like joggers before a run, then converging on the melee. Soon seven wolves were milling and leaping at Female Four. One of the younger wolves was ejected from the writhing mass. He walked a few yards away, raised his head, and emitted a series of high yips, a pitiful imitation of a howl.

Unpracticed as his performance was, its effect was immediate. Two other wolves left the tumble, sat, and began to howl. Soon all eight wolves were howling in an atonal chorus that built and echoed. It was a Schönberg concerto with cadenzas by Coltrane. When it ended, the wolves began to disperse.

As the howl faded into the trees, a small crowd of people began to gather, shouting inanities at the wolves and shrieking at them to get them to howl again—but when a howling session is over, as this one was, wolves enter a fifteen-minute refractory period during which nothing in the world can get them to howl again. Some speculate that the function of the refractory period is to allow all the packs in an area to hear each other. By remaining silent after a howl and listening for replies, a pack can learn where other packs in the vicinity are.

Among the last to join the crowd at the fence was an

eight-year-old boy whose cunning little outfit had, I was sure, graced the pages of a recent issue of the *New Yorker*. He turned to his father and, pointing to the sign identifying the wolves, piped, "Look, Daddy, wolves."

The father replied, "No, Kent, those aren't wolves. Wolves don't look like dogs—they're big and mean."

Daddy dragged Kent off just as Female Four moved slowly to the top of the mound, her retinue in procession behind her. The wolves lined up on the mound forming a perfect row, all staring at the gate. It was feeding time. Lisa Baer glided up in her golf cart, said a quick hello, and began to scribble. Male Four trotted to the gate as the keeper arrived and followed her to the area in front of the mound. She threw chunks of turkey to the wolves on the mound, then handed the last chunk to Male Four, who kept it between his jaws as he escorted her to the gate. He ate half, then carried the other half to the den, disappeared inside, and reappeared two seconds later without it. For a moment I imagined the old wolf lying in the den, watching shadows on the wall, blinded by the light whenever he looked outside.

Soon all the wolves were lying in the sun, oblivious to the howls, catcalls, and insults of the visitors. The show was over.

Perhaps it was only because I didn't know the wolves well enough, but it seemed that dominance was much more important at the Chicago Zoo than at Joe's. It was the dominant pair that escorted the keeper in and out at mealtime and that produced most of the scent marks I saw. The power of rank was dramatically illustrated on that last afternoon, when Female Four froze a large young male in his tracks merely by raising her head off her paws and glancing in his direction. He was more than fifteen yards away, but he put his tail down, his ears back, and skulked away to sulk behind a bush.

As clouds piled up in the west, the wolves flopped down one by one, needing only brandy and cigars to complete the image of postprandial contentment. When the rain began, they paid it no attention, snoozing on as chilly rivulets ran off their backs. I was not so well protected, and my notes began to turn to paste. It was time to get back to Ann Arbor. I gathered my gear and squished off to my vehicle. I turned to wave, but the wolves ignored me. To them I was just another nameless visitor.

CHAPTER ELEVEN
Hunger Makes the Wolf
CHARLES BERGMAN

CHARLES BERGMAN *received his doctorate from the University of Minnesota. He has written on environmental topics for such magazines as* National Geographic, Audubon, *and* Smithsonian. *He is professor of English at Pacific Lutheran University and lives in northern Washington. His book* Wild Echoes: Encounters with the Most Endangered Animals in North America (1990) *describes the plight of endangered species, which he defines as "broken creatures, haunting the margins of our lives . . . less a part of nature than of our culture."*

AFTER ALL MY TRAVELING in North America, looking for wolves, the central question remains: What place will we make for the wolf in our culture? In our lives?

The wolf, like other big predators, evokes powerful fears and intense passions. Like grizzly bears and mountain lions, the wolf poses major challenges: Will we preserve what range it has left in the United States? Will we reintroduce it into parts of its historic range in the contiguous United States? I had two very different encounters with adult wolves in the wild, and they suggest two poles in our experience of these predators—two postures we can take.

In late April 1985, I flew to the Eureka Weather Station, on Ellesmere Island, because this was reported to be the best place in the High Arctic to see the arctic race of wolf, *Canis lupus arctos*. At 80° north latitude, it is a place that would appeal to any imagination in love with extremes. I went with a friend and photographer.

Located on the Fosheim Peninsula, the Canadian weather station where we stayed looked out on Slidre Fiord, a small arm off the Eureka Sound. In the afternoon, I could walk westward out over the ice on the fiord, to the edge of the sound, and see Axel Heiberg Island rolling into high hills in the cold, diaphanous light. The sun no longer set at night but rolled around the sky like a glowing ring, turning the snow and the arctic foxes into pastel shades of pink in its low and slanting light. But the cold was still strong. Icebergs lay trapped in the frozen fiord like huge hulks, images of arrested motion, as if the world had simply ground down to a halt.

On my walks around the island, I felt as though I had come to the edge of some austere absolutes—intense cold, a timeless and blinding light, immeasurable miles of blank snow. A white silence brooded over the ice and snow. There isn't that much snow on Ellesmere—in the polar desert, it gets about 15 inches a year, which doesn't melt until June. It was an immense void, swept clean and empty by the wind. I found myself thinking of arctic explorers, and of how some people will go such a long way to get a glimpse of the untouched and the ultimate.

It would be easy to romanticize my trip to Eureka, but that would be partly illusion. Other compelling images remain. The weather-station compound reminded me vaguely of a sprawling, self-contained cocoon: low buildings hunkered against the cold. The main building, where the six or so men lived while stationed at Eureka, was a vast dormitory complex with all the current accoutrements of comfort: wide-screen TV, VCR, library of movies (I saw *The Right Stuff* and *Gorky Park* while I was there), pool table, weight room. There was also a full-time cook and baker who kept us supplied with more food than we could eat—huge meals and a constant spread of cakes and cookies. I felt less that I was confronting the remote High Arctic than that I was insulated from it.

The first night, after dinner, one of the guys offered to give us a ride to the dump. Arctic wolves hang out there, feeding off the garbage.

We scraped our leftovers into a bunch of plastic buckets, loaded them into the back of a pickup, and drove up the small hill between the bunkhouse, the airport runway, and the dump. We drove slowly, honking the horn like mad.

Looking at our right, out over the fiord, I spotted three white wolves a few hundred yards away. They moved superbly, their legs barely moving, in an ankle trot. Against the cool white world of ice and snow, they were like white ghosts, like white shadows even, drifting by.

A Russian proverb says, "The wolf is fed by its feet." Wolves travel all winter, and the urge to travel is probably related to the need to hunt. The wolf's chest is narrow and strong, its legs are long, and its paws are huge—all adaptations for a life on the move, even through deep winter snow. A wolf can cover a mile in about five minutes, effortlessly it seems, and keep the pace up for hours. It can cover up to 120 miles per day. When it spots quarry, the wolf prefers a short chase, a quick burst of about 100 yards, lips curled back, fangs out, snarling and barking.

When the three wolves heard us blasting away on the horn, they bolted toward us as if it were a hunt. All three of them caught up with us, fell in behind the truck, and followed us to the dump. I have vivid memories, poignant yet almost comical, of us driving, the horn blaring, and the wild wolves racing behind the truck like Pavlovian dogs after their dinner, ears pressed back against their heads, big snouts and heads pressed forward, long legs bounding under arching white backs.

At the garbage dump, we emptied the buckets and retreated. The wolves went straight for the food. Up close, through binoculars, their snouts and paws were smudged and greasy from eating at the dump, their white coats bleary with soot.

These were not the wild wolves I had come so far to see. Though they were wild, they seemed nearly tame. I found in these wolves an example of one way the Western mind accommodates all those disturbing impulses we find in the wolf—sex and violence, wildness and passion. We train it. We control it, as we "control" the wolves of Alaska. Both the literal and the symbolic wolf are left to live along the margins of our lives, feeding on our leftovers, as it were. It was a sad image, an image of loss.

But I have another image of wolves that counters this one and reveals a different way of relating to wolves. It comes from the den I watched with Danny Grangaard in the mountains around Tok, Alaska. The one I crawled into. The one where I watched the pups. The one where I got the urge to see the mother wolf.

After watching the den from the blind for some time, we decided we weren't going to see the parents come in while we were so close. Wild wolves are elusive. You have to be extremely clever, and lucky, to see one. Danny suggested we go up onto a bluff above the den, where we could camp and watch without the wolves' seeing, smelling, or hearing us. The bluff was very high, several hundred feet, and overlooked a gravel bar and several small ponds along Bone Creek. We made our camp under several big spruce trees. From our campfire, we could watch the bar below, though the actual den was out of sight in the trees.

We watched for four days, an almost constant vigil. I knew the scene below by heart. I could close my eyes and picture the creek entering the open gravel bar, rushing past and bending right in the distance between two very steep slopes that led straight up to mountain peaks. In my mind's eye, I knew just where the poplars were, at the base of the bluff; I could see the line of spring-fed ponds on the right, like milky-blue beads on a string, full of Dolly Varden rippling the surface as they fed in the evenings. Several times, I even imagined seeing an adult wolf step out of the bush and onto the clearing of the gravel bar. The watching only intensified my desire to see the mother wolf.

At three in the morning of the fourth night, a wolf woke me with its howling. I'd never heard anything like it before; its eerie notes were emphasized by the remote mountains and the smoldering ember of our fire. The howl was a manic moaning, rising and falling in pitch until it trailed off on a haunted, mournful note. I sat up in my sleeping bag and woke Danny.

A wolf howls to assert territory, to call meetings with other wolves, to entertain itself, or, as this one seemed to be doing, to announce its presence. Deep in the Alaska Range, the bluff was ringed with rugged peaks. Sky-piercing and heart-piercing, snow-veined relentless peaks. The howls and the mountains—all around, the beauty of the unattainable. In the slow alembic of a pale summer dawn, the snowcaps glowed in Botticellean blues and pinks. From the den below, the pups answered the adult's howl, a yapping chorus, more tremulous and piercingly high-pitched. The pups whined like a pack of coyotes. The adult answered them. The howls rolled down the mountainsides, echoing off the buttes and rock spires, the talus and cliffs, spilling out of distant recesses and inhuman reaches.

This was a true waking, wolf howls washing over me in waves, to something wild and summer-new.

Danny looked at me across the campfire. "If you're gonna see a wild wolf, this is your chance."

We got up, stood out on the bluff, and scanned the bar. Both of us breathed shallow, short heaves of expectation, alive to the imminent promise of satisfied hopes. And then the wolf appeared on the gravel bar in the grayish shadows below. She stepped from the greenish puff of aspens into the open, walking slowly, aimlessly, nonchalantly.

"That's the bitch," Danny whispered. He'd seen her several times before. She was all white, except for a steel-gray saddle on her haunches.

A few feet onto the gravel, she stopped and looked back over her shoulder, Bette Davis style, toward the den. She sniffed the air, padded on across the bar to the right, and wandered slowly toward our bluff. Her indolence was delicious to watch. Almost out of sight, she stopped, raised her snout, and howled again, a kind of hysteria in the voice so at odds with her casual pace.

And as if she were merely a specter, she vanished as phantomlike as she had appeared, into the timber at the base of the bluff.

Danny and I had been a rapt audience. A wild wolf. We can make room for them; we can let them live their own lives. The howl of the wolf speaks of regions in nature, and in ourselves, that we can never tame, never control. But we can learn to live with it. Occasionally, even if for only a few minutes, we can hear that demonic music in their howls, feel the ecstasy of those haunting echoes.

On the bluff, after she had gone, I let myself go in delirious surrender. I had gotten what I wanted, a look at the mother wolf. Sometimes we do get what we want; sometimes what is given is enough—like a mother/lover's breast in my mouth. Dancing like a dervish, lost in the euphoria of release, I was caught up in a sort of wolf madness, celebrating a wild wolf, feeling less like a spectator than, suddenly, a partner with this mother wolf in a dance I didn't for a minute understand.

CHAPTER TWELVE

Lobo, King of the Currumpaw

ERNEST THOMPSON SETON

ERNEST THOMPSON SETON *was born in England
in 1860. He studied art in Paris for four years before
moving to the United States, where he became one of the
earliest popular writers of nature stories. While he was
often criticized for presenting overly anthropomorphic views
of animals, his books helped to awaken the public to the
plight of animals everywhere. Seton's involvement in the
killing of the famed wolf Lobo resulted in his viewing
wolves in a new light. He hoped that his account of the
death of Lobo would aid in educating the public, and
wrote, "I have tried to stop the stupid and brutal work of
destruction by an appeal—not to reason, that has failed
hitherto—but to sympathy, and especially the sympathies
of the coming generation." His books include* Wild
Animals I Have Known *(1898),* Biography of a
Grizzly *(1900), and* The Lives of the Hunted
*(1901). In 1928, Seton was awarded the
John Burroughs Medal. He died in 1946.*

YEARS AGO a friend who owned a cattle ranch in the
Currumpaw Valley of northern New Mexico, and who
knew that I had once been a wolf hunter, urged me to
come there and rid the region of a marauding pack of
gray wolves which, in defiance of local trappers and
cowboys, was taking a terrible toll of valuable cattle. I
was in the Southwest at the time and I accepted the invitation, setting out for the Currumpaw with a wagon

and team, two helpers—Billy Allen and Charley Winn—and some wolf traps.

On my arrival I learned that the pack was led by a giant wolf which local Mexicans had named Old Lobo, the King. All the ranchmen knew Lobo well, though few had ever seen him. His voice, an octave lower than that of his fellows, was unmistakable, and his track was easily recognized. An ordinary wolf's forefoot is four and a half inches long; Lobo's was five and a half. The old outlaw's wiliness and strength were in proportion to his size. Under his diabolically cunning leadership the pack avoided all efforts to poison or trap them. The ranchmen had finally set a price of a thousand dollars on Lobo's head—an unparalleled wolf-bounty. But he and his band seemed to possess charmed lives, and in five years had destroyed more than two thousand cattle. They were so fastidious about what they ate that they touched nothing except the tenderest parts of yearling heifers, one of which they killed almost every night.

Lobo feared only one thing—firearms. Knowing that all men in that region carried them, he would never face a human being, and permitted his band to roam abroad only after nightfall. For such an adversary the traps I had brought were too small, and pending the arrival of larger ones, I tried to get him with poison. For bait, I cooked a mixture of cheese and kidney fat from a freshly killed heifer. To avoid tainting it with the odor of man I wore a pair of gloves steeped in the hot blood of the heifer, and was even careful not to breathe upon the meat. After it cooled I cut it into lumps with a bone knife and inserted in each lump an odorless capsule of strychnine and cyanide, sealing it with a bit of the cheese. I put this bait into a rawhide bag rubbed all over with the blood, and rode forth on horseback, dragging the bag at the end of a rope. Making a ten-mile circuit, I dropped a lump every quarter of a mile, taking care not to touch it with bare hands.

Next day I rode the circuit, eager to learn the result. From the wolves' tracks in the dust I found that they had scented my drag and had followed it. At the spot where I had dropped the first piece of bait, Lobo had sniffed about and had finally picked it up. Now, I thought, I've got him. But I could see no dead wolf on the plain. Proceeding to the second and third baits, I found that they also were gone. At the next one I discovered what had happened. Lobo had not eaten the baits but had *carried them in his mouth* and dropped them when he came to the fourth. There he scattered filth all over them to express his utter contempt for all my stratagems.

Obviously the King was too clever to be taken with poison, so I obtained a hundred heavy, double-spring steel wolf traps. My helpers and I worked a week to set them out properly in all the trails leading to the watering places and canyon crossings of the region. Each trap was chained to a short log and rubbed with fresh blood; at strategic spots I buried four traps about a foot from each other. I placed the logs on each side of the trail, and after concealing them with dust and grass we smoothed the ground with the body of a rabbit. The traps were so well hidden that no man could have detected them even in daylight, but Lobo was not fooled.

When I inspected my traps a few days later I read again, from the tracks in the dust, the record of his doings. When he had come upon the first trap his keen nose had warned him that there was something suspicious ahead. Cautiously scratching around, he had exposed trap, chain and log. Then, passing on, he had treated a dozen more traps in the same manner.

Studying his moves, I found that when he detected a trap he invariably moved off the trail to the downwind side. That gave me a new idea. Setting one trap directly in the trail, I placed three others on each side of it, forming an H. Now, I thought, when he comes to the middle trap which forms the crossbar of the H, he will certainly get into one of the side traps. But he was too smart. Upon encountering the trap in the trail, being warned of it by his incredible sense of smell, he had stopped. Then, instead of moving off to one side as was his custom, he had *backed up, carefully putting each paw in its old track,* until he was beyond dangerous ground. Once clear, he had made a wide circuit around my H— and had triumphantly gone on to kill another heifer a few miles away.

For four months I pursued the wily old reprobate and his band, to no avail. I was at my wit's end. And he might have roamed and marauded to the end of his natural span if he had not made a mistake—the one mistake of his life. He married a young and incautious wife. Some Mexicans, who occasionally caught glimpses of the pack, told me his mate was pure white. They called her Blanca.

Now at last I believed I had found a weak spot in the

old warrior's armor and planned my strategy for a final campaign. Killing a heifer, I placed two traps near the carcass so they would be fairly obvious, then cut off the head and laid it on the ground a short distance away, as if it had been carelessly thrown aside. To it I fastened two deodorized traps and buried them. I then brushed the ground smooth with the skin of a coyote and made tracks over the trap with one of its paws.

The next morning, to my delight, the head was gone. The tracks revealed that Lobo had come, decoyed by the delicious odor of fresh beef. He had walked around the carcass at a safe distance. The rest of the pack, except one, had sensed his usual warning and had stayed away from the spot. That one—a small wolf—had heedlessly trotted over to examine the beef head, had set foot in one of my traps, and had run off, dragging head and all.

About a mile away we overtook the hapless wolf. It was Blanca! She was the handsomest wolf I had ever seen. Lobo was with her, and only when he saw men coming with guns did he leave her. Making off up a hill, he called to her to follow, but the horns of the big beef head caught in the rocks and held her. Turning to fight, she raised her voice in a long howl that rolled over the canyon. From far away came Lobo's deep response. That was her last call; quickly we closed in on her and killed her and rode back to the ranch with her body.

All that day we heard Lobo calling. It was no longer the old, defiant howl; there was a note of sorrow in it now. As evening fell, his voice sounded nearer and I could tell that he was not far from the place where we had overtaken Blanca. When he reached the spot where his mate had died, he seemed to know what had happened and his wailing was piteous to hear. Even the stolid cowboys said they had "never heard a wolf carry on like that before." In the night Lobo followed the tracks of our horses almost to the ranch house, and next morning we found our watchdog torn to bits.

I went feverishly to work to catch him before he might abandon his search for Blanca. My helpers and I placed traps in sets of four on every trail leading to the home canyon. Each was fastened to a log, every log-and-trap was buried, and with one of Blanca's paws I made tracks over every trap-set. The second day afterward I saw a great gray form in a trail of the north canyon. There, helpless, lay the King of the Currumpaw. He had come to the tracks I had made with Blanca's forefoot, and had forgotten his customary caution.

When he saw me, the old hero—worn out from struggling for two days and nights—arose valiantly to give battle. His eyes glared green with fury and his powerful jaws snapped viciously as he tried to reach me and my trembling horse. But the traps held him fast and, weak from hunger and loss of blood, he soon sank down exhausted. Now that I had him at last, pity came over me. "You grand old outlaw," I said, "I'm sorry to do it, but it must be done." I threw my lasso, but as the noose was dropping on his neck he seized it and with one chop cut the thick rope. I had my rifle but did not wish to spoil his royal hide, so I galloped back to the house to get another lasso—and Billy Allen. We flung a stick to the wolf and before he could drop it our lassos tightened on his neck. It was easy to lash his jaws tight over the stick with a rope.

As soon as he was bound he made no further resistance and uttered no sound. He merely looked at me calmly as if to say, "You have got me at last; do as you please with me." From that time on he took no further notice of us. We tied his legs and released the traps. Our strength was just sufficient to lift his 150-pound weight across my saddle. At the ranch house I put a strong collar on his neck, fastened it to a post by means of a chain and removed his bonds. I put meat and water beside him but he paid no heed. He did not even move a muscle when I touched him, but turned his head away, gazing past me down the canyon to the open plains—the kingdom where he had so long hunted and triumphed. Thus he lay until sundown.

It is said that a lion shorn of his strength, an eagle robbed of his freedom or a dove bereft of his mate will die of a broken heart. Who will say that this grim bandit could bear the loss of all three? This only I know: When morning came he was lying just as I had left him; but his spirit was gone—the king-wolf was dead. A cowboy helped me carry him into the shed where the remains of Blanca lay. As we placed Lobo beside her, the cattleman looked down at him and said, "There— you *would* come to her; now you are together again."

CHAPTER THIRTEEN

Las Margaritas

DAVID E. BROWN

DAVID E. BROWN *was born in 1938 and received a degree in wildlife conservation and management from San Jose State College in California. He has spent over thirty years with the Arizona Game and Fish Department, and in 1980 became a big game supervisor with that agency. He has published numerous articles on wildlife conservation, and is a fellow with the Arizona-Nevada Academy of Science.*

LAS MARGARITAS was the name McBride gave to a wolf that operated over a large territory from the Zacatecas-Durango border through almost the entire state of Durango. McBride (1980) described an episode that began during the late 1960s when this wolf started killing yearling steers and heifers at Las Margaritas Ranch. The wolf was missing two toes from its left front foot, and its experience with traps left a memory that served it well; all efforts to poison or trap this wolf were futile. In spring 1970, Las Margaritas moved north to the Mazatlán-Durango Highway and began killing steers on the El Carmen and Santa Barbara ranches on the west side of the railroad between Durango and Regocijo. McBride, trapping in Durango for the Cattlemen's Union, had heard about this wolf when he was trying to catch a pair of yearling wolves. By March he had taken the yearling female, and the male had gone. Las Margaritas then came to McBride.

In April depredations started again; McBride at first thought the young male had returned; but when he saw the track in a dusty trail, he noticed the missing toes—trademark of Las Margaritas. After reportedly killing thirteen steers, the wolf went west in May and, after killing more cattle, disappeared. In June Las Margaritas returned to Rancho Santa Barbara where it killed eighteen steers. Characteristically, the wolf seldom used the same trail twice. If it came into a pasture by a log road, it left by a cow trail.

McBride was certain he could catch the wolf if he could get it near a trap. Finally, at the end of July, the wolf came down a washed-out log road and passed one of McBride's trap sets. The wolf smelled the trap, turned back, and trotted up to it, barely missing the trigger with the gap caused by the missing toes. The wolf then apparently suspected the trap and left the road. It did not return until September; ninety-six steers and yearling heifers were reported killed in the next eight months on one ranch alone.

In October McBride found where Las Margaritas had urinated on a small juniper beside a logging road; he carefully placed a set there. Two weeks later the wolf passed by the trap, advanced a few steps towards it, and then ran down the road. The only scent on the bush was its own, and McBride could not understand how the wolf knew the trap was there. Las Margaritas then moved to a new area where it resumed killing.

A pair of wolves showed up in this area in November and began killing in the same pasture in which Las Margaritas was operating. Several days after their arrival, McBride picked up fresh tracks that the two wolves had made before the dew. He also saw Las Margaritas' tracks but they were made after the dew had formed. While trailing them, McBride noted that whenever the male of the pair left the road to make a scent station, Las Margaritas never investigated but continued down the road. Finally, the pair of wolves came to one of McBride's traps, and the female was caught. When Las Margaritas came to where the trap had been pulled out of the ground, the wolf left the road and disappeared until December.

In late December reports of Las Margaritas' killings began anew, but in a different pasture. Traps were set daily on all the wolf's travel routes, but again the wolf seldom returned to a previously used trail. In January McBride made three blind sets in a narrow cow trail in the gap of a mountain, convinced that the wolf would not go to any baited site. Two weeks passed before Las Margaritas came down the mountain divide and hit the cow trails about a hundred yards above the traps. About fifteen feet from the first trap, she left the trail and went around the set. Large evergreen oaks were on either side of the trail, and windblown leaves hid the traps. McBride had stepped from his horse to a steer hide while setting the traps, the dirt had been removed by a sifter, and the traps had been boiled in oak leaves. The trap could not have been better concealed. Nonetheless, the wolf returned to the trail without being caught and approached the second set on the other side of a pine tree that had fallen across the trail. Again the wolf left the trail and went around the trap. As it neared the third trap, the wolf left the trail before getting to the trap site. On trailing up the trap, McBride later found a coyote in it. The wolf had left, and for about a week nothing was heard of Las Margaritas until it began killing about fifteen miles to the west. By March, McBride was convinced that he would never catch this wolf.

At times, McBride noticed that Las Margaritas had investigated a campfire along the road where log truck drivers would stop and cook. He decided to set a trap near a road that the wolf was sure to come down if it continued to kill in this pasture. He built a fire over the trap and let it burn out. At the edge of the ashes he placed a piece of dried skunk hide.

On March 15 the wolf came down the road, winded the ashes and skunk hide, and walked over to investigate. Las Margaritas was caught by the crippled foot and the trap held. There was much celebration among the ranchers the following day. In eleven months of intensive effort and several thousand miles on horseback, McBride had managed to get the wolf near a trap only four times.

CHAPTER FOURTEEN

A Song of the Kitiwanga

ROBERT FRANKLIN LESLIE

ROBERT FRANKLIN LESLIE *was born in Texas in 1911.*
He received a bachelor of arts at Santa Barbara State
College and a master's degree in botanical ecology from
the University of Southern California. His love of wild
places is shown by his many trips to the wilderness areas of
Canada, the United States, and Mexico. He spent thirty
years as a teacher, and later lectured widely on ecology and
photography. His books include Read the Wild Water
(1966), High Trails West *(1967), and* Wild Courage
(1974). Perhaps his best-known book is The Bears and I
(1968), which was fictionalized as a Walt Disney
motion picture. He lives in southern California.

ALL THE WOLVES were gaunt and knotty from late-summer molt, particularly the younger ones, who had undergone a strenuous apprenticeship with their elders. Training had begun, of course, as soon as the young-sters' teeth were ready. However, the young wolves had to be prepared to accompany Náhani and perform pack duties during rigorous winter hunting. Therefore, their elders had driven them to the brink of their endurance in late summer and early autumn.

They learned hunting techniques based on tracking and exhausting the largest animals in the western hemi-sphere. Parents trained subyearlings to be vigilant, to take advantage of the camouflage of their coats when stalking, and to recognize every familiar as well as foreign forest scent. They mastered the message carried by tracks and paw prints. Attentive youngsters learned the art of killing and skinning a porcupine. Those parents who were the most dedicated teachers insured that their offspring would survive, should separation from the pack occur. Náhani would teach the teamwork required in running the open-end horseshoe formation for herding prey into ravines and other close quarters for quicker, more certain kills.

While other animals were preoccupied with storing up fat for the winter, the wolves feasted upon a bounteous berry crop. They dug rhizomes and bulbs, grazed late bunchgrass, munched wood sorrel and cranberries, and gnawed sweetbark and bitterberry branches. From the first quarter of the Sagamore-Council-Moon until far into the Moon-of-Painted-Leaves they became vegetarians. On occasion ravens tried to lead the family teams to nearby prey for a co-operative feast during those annual meatless weeks prior to organized autumn hunting, but to no avail. In fact, during this vigorous yearling training, when the wolves selected deer and elk for attack, the animals were released at the end of the "exercise" with only minor wounds. The wolves were densely furred nonhibernators, preying upon nonhibernators, and there was no reason for them to accumulate layers of fat against the winter months.

After the training period, all wolves resumed their regular routines. They took advantage of every possible sunny hour on the rimrock. During the dark of the moon, Greg and Náhani spent from eight to ten hours a day on alpine heaths not far from the pack.

With the waxing September Moon-of-Painted-Leaves, moaning chinooks herded sheeplike formations of clouds across the sky and soughed night and day throughout the conifer forest around the choppy lake. When a slow wedge of southing swans crossed the sky one afternoon, Greg moved into the lean-to and collected a supply of dry firewood. Time was running out. He fought desperately to hold back the clock.

The first general storm hammered against the Kitiwanga's enormous, malleable mass. For three days and nights the tempest raged; rain cascaded over the lake; lightning constantly whittled at sullen crests. Ancient spruce, long overmature, crashed to the forest floor to become tomorrow's nourishing duff. Even during the most truculent squalls, the wolves rolled in mud, played up and down the beach, then bathed in the lake to drown their ectoparasites before returning to the dens. Náhani, dripping wet and smelling like new-cut wheat, came to Greg's lean-to day and night. She had begun to spend entire nights curled up alongside his sleeping bag while the wolf families had been away training the young. She continued the habit after their return. Somewhere, instinctively, she too must have known that time was running out.

On the morning after the storm, the north wind rolled the remaining cloud curtain back toward the Pacific. Most of the pack, led at full canter by the chief hunters, headed down the creek toward the Gataga River canyon. Náhani, on the other hand, indicated that Greg should escort her on an inspection trip along the north shore. A flight of shrikes, landing in two inches of water and taking to the air again at regular intervals, continually announced the position of man and wolf to the wild community. For some reason Náhani had sent her bodyguard with the pack. Since the wolves were invading territory defended by other packs, the guards might be sorely needed on the Gataga foray.

At a point where a fault line of upended limestone strata forced a detour into the forest, Náhani preceded Greg along the base of the extruded rock ledge all the way to the north rim of the Denetiah trough. At timber line they came upon an excavation, obviously the den of a resident coyote family. Toothing bones, scats, and other fresh refuse lay scattered about the mound at the tunnel's opening.

Náhani stopped in her tracks. The crest hair on her neck and withers suddenly resembled a mane, and the long jowl hair stood straight out to make her face look twice as wide below the eyes. Rising and falling dewlaps and a backward flick of one ear signaled that Greg should remain motionless. He had never received that signal. Intuitively, he understood her meaning, having become sensitive to so many wolf signals. He watched her tense her hocks and pasterns. She spread her feet and barked, as only leader wolves do.

Nothing happened immediately. Then a drowsy male coyote walked slowly from the mouth of the tunnel. He took one look at Náhani and yawned extravagantly. Here was the first creature, Greg thought, to exhibit such a casual attitude toward Náhani. The two animals padded slowly in circles around each other, sniffling rear ends cautiously but with no apparent hostility. Obviously they were more than nodding acquaintances. Náhani stood forty inches high at the withers, was six feet two inches long from the tip of her nose to the base of her tail, and weighed more than eleven stones. She was almost twice the size of the coyote and four times his weight. Yet it was clear that the coyote neither owed nor paid homage to Náhani, the queen wolf.

When the coyote scented Greg, he dove deep into his tunnel. As Náhani continued on the inspection trip, Greg paused to compare her six-inch track with the two-inch coyote print.

Náhani quickened her gait along the steep hillside. Greg had to run to keep up. He could find no explanation for her sudden burst of energy, but sensed her urgency. Often she looked back to be sure he was still following.

Abruptly, Náhani stood alert. The main crest of the limestone fault disappeared under a quarter mile of grassy brae, a narrow belt of windy moorland between the lake basin's evergreen forest and the lofty alpine zone of frost-twisted subtundra. There was a gritty dryness to the air. In these austere barrows there were only two seasons: six weeks of spring and forty-six weeks of winter.

White ptarmigans, whose bronze-and-orange-spotted feathers looked as if they were blotched with caribou lichen, stood on rocky outcroppings, thumping their wings in muffled unison. Fattening marmots whistled from sunny rockeries, obviously annoying the ptarmigans. A mother coyote appeared to be teaching her young to search out the silent, motionless chick ptarmigans. However, the pups were displaying greater interest in the plentiful supply of currants and *olallie*, the upland huckleberry. Then several yearling coyotes suddenly flashed across the heath and graphically demonstrated that they had learned their mother's techniques for stalking marmots and ptarmigan.

Náhani turned her head. She looked Greg squarely in the eye, a penetrating, thoughtful look as if to say, "To a coyote your violets and avalanche lilies cannot compare with the smell of ptarmigan and marmot!"

Greg put his arm around her neck. She licked the perspiration from his forehead and temples. More than ever Greg realized that understanding between him and the wolf was due in part to his Indian willingness to go along with her animal wildness, to the humility he always felt in her presence, and to an unexplored part of himself that was still primitive animal.

By now the sun was lowering behind the saw-toothed Cassiars. The air had chilled. Without disturbing the coyotes, Náhani indicated that Greg should follow her back down the hill. She had known all along where the coyotes were and what they were doing. Something deep within her animal mind had compelled her to take her friend to watch the spectacle.

▪

Long before they reached camp that evening, Náhani conveyed a feeling that something was wrong. She kept looking back at Greg, urging greater speed down the north-shore beach. She barked, whined, or howled as she ran. She was clearly on edge. Upon smoothly packed cobble and sand the barefoot young Indian was scarcely able to keep up with the powerful wolf. Four large males ran to meet them when they were within a mile of the denning complex. Her "staff officers" reflected distress.

Náhani and her four "lieutenants" plunged through the outlet flume. Then she inched carefully across the strip of beach, as though afraid and enraged at the same time.

The entire pack stood in trembling assembly at the log in front of Greg's camp.

■

Náhani shouldered her way to the center of the tightly compressed group. The four solemn dog wolves assumed guard positions outside the jostling corps. Greg waded the creek and slowly started across the fifty yards of sand and cobble between the outlet and his camp. He saw Náhani's long, white nose lift above the milling forms, heard her low moan that triggered high-pitched wails from every throat.

For a time Greg debated whether or not to go nearer. Ordinarily, clusters of the kennel moved quickly aside whenever he walked toward them. But now the picture had changed. As Greg stepped cautiously forward, the wolves' mournful cries dropped several octaves, and became deep, threatening snarls. In the rapidly gathering dusk, the circle of wolves swarmed and shifted so restlessly that he was unable to appraise the situation.

Suddenly Náhani's hackled white back moved away from the center of the pack. Stepping slightly aside, she barked. The wolves slowly separated into groups of twos, threes, and fours. With bared, flashing fangs they howled and chomped, seemingly directing their rage toward Greg for something he did not yet understand.

Then he saw the fallen wolf. Panting on the white sand within a few feet of the camp log, lay one of the small mates of the bigamous male that had been injured in the fight over the elk carcass. Greg remembered the times he had fished and cooked for that family while the kennel patrolled the forage-range runway. He had deep affection for those two females, the only wolves in the pack besides Náhani that would allow him to touch them. Two inches above the pastern, the small female's right rear shank was firmly clamped between the jaws of a Number 4 double-spring steel trap.

Where had she stepped into that trap? And why with the *hind* foot? How had she managed to unstaple the trap from its anchoring clog and carry it back to Greg's camp?

The wolves, including Náhani, reached a peak of anger Greg had not believed possible in the so-called "lower" animals. He had never looked upon wolves for what legend reputed them to be, but for what they meant to him. And now for the first time in his life, he knew—as an animal in danger would know—the meaning of fear.

Instinctively, and from bitter experience, the wolves associated the man smell with the steel smell of traps. Náhani, who at that moment stood at the head of their ranks and glared at Greg, carried a mutilated right front paw as a result of the combination of man and steel.

Greg realized that if he failed to face the wolves down, if he failed to communicate, his life would end in a matter of seconds. Without faltering, he walked rapidly toward the trapped wolf. He never once took his gaze from Náhani's icy stare.

The fleeting thought of the man smell—the *Indian* man smell—crossed his mind. Since the day when the Canadian Indian took up the white man's trapping tools, wolves had associated agony with the *Indian* man smell. Greg hesitated for a moment, sensing that the wolves were aware of his fear. And that very fear may have saved his life. His entire body exuded perspiration: chief source of the man smell they hated and shunned. Human feces and urine somehow hold no terror for the wolf, but perspiration is another matter. Greg would only hope that Náhani would now accept *his* man smell.

■

"Náhani!" Greg shouted. "I'm coming through!"

At the sound of his voice every wolf between him and the trapped female stepped aside and was instantly silent. But the victim quickly struggled to her feet. She lifted the trapped leg so that nothing but the three-foot chain dragged the ground as she hobbled away on three legs to her den. Her mate, the other female, and Náhani disappeared into the same tunnel. Not a wolf remained in sight. Greg stepped over the camp log, sat down, and cupped his hands over his face.

During those first moments after the confrontation, he was too upset to think clearly. He could think of no way to remove that trap before the wolves began to chew away the leg above the steel jaws. It would be no simple task. That female, while somewhat smaller than the average British Columbia timber wolf, could sever the human jugular vein and tear out the windpipe with a single snap of her jaws. Although insane with fear, shock, rage, pain, and fatigue, the wolf could still react with more deadly swiftness than any North American predator.

Deep in the cramped quarters of a den—possibly in the presence of several hostile wolves—the task of removing the trap would be many times more difficult than it would have been on the beach.

All through the long night he waited for Náhani. She did not come to his camp. Before retiring to the sleeping bag, he took the flashlight and went to the opening of the little female's den. Fifteen feet inside the entrance the tunnel made a right-angle turn, beyond which Greg was unable to see. The only sign of life from within was a faint, recurrent sobbing.

As he lay facing the stars, Greg tried to reconstruct the events of the day. The pack had left early, possibly to search lowland bogs for late-ripening berries, possibly to poach game along a weaker neighbor's runway. The wolves had traveled a minimum of fifteen miles by the time they reached the Gataga River. Even if the female had stepped into the trap at the point of confluence of Denetiah Creek and the Gataga, fifteen miles was a long way to hobble on three paws and carry the painful trap and chain on the fourth.

To each species, Greg thought, the Earth Mother has

given some kind of armor to withstand her rigorous disciplines—but nature has never reckoned with traps and guns.

Greg awakened at sunrise. His urgency to remove the trap was spurred by Náhani's serious expression as she looked down at him from the log. There had been no serenades to greet the dawn. Greg rushed to her and examined her muzzle and brisket. No blood. She licked the stubble of whiskers that covered his chin.

He thanked Gitche Manito that she was still his friend.

The air was warm. He put on a pair of shorts, fixed a quick breakfast of corn-meal mush and dried milk, then rushed to the den. He held a flashlight in one hand, a pan of reconstituted milk in the other. Náhani reached the entrance before he did.

From the size of the dirt mound on the hillside below the tunnel entrance, he estimated that the whelping chamber lay about twenty feet beyond and slightly higher than the opening. The soil, a light sandy loam containing much glacial detritus and scratchy-barked roots, had caved in several times since the family had dug the den.

Greg listened. The faintest whine reached his ears each time he imitated a wolf sound for soothing or calling, but neither he nor Náhani could persuade the wolf to come out.

Greg always felt claustrophobic in dark, close places. Weather and insects permitting, he generally slept on the *outside* of his sleeping bag. Now he dreaded the thought of crawling into the crumbly tunnel. Yet under the circumstances, he had no choice. If he built a smoke fire, the wolf would simply rush out and enter another den. If the tunnel caved in, he would suffocate within four or five minutes.

He placed his flashlight and a pan of milk in the tunnel beyond the entrance, and tried to squeeze through. His broad, naked shoulders were too wide. With a leather thong he tied his shoulder-length hair behind his head. With his side knife he enlarged the entrance and cleared away the dirt and rock. The tunnel was slightly larger in diameter than the entrance; but in order to inch along on his belly, he had to extend his arms full length ahead, pull with his hands, and push with his feet. Even so, when he took a deep breath of the rapidly fouling air, his chest completely filled the tunnel cavity. Apparently the wolves felt secure in such close quarters.

When he reached the turn in the tunnel, he flashed a beam of light into the whelping chamber at the far end. In a choking explosion of loose hair and dust, the male and the other female shot from the chamber into another tunnel with a secret opening somewhere in the hillside forest. Greg tried to back up but found it physically impossible to move backward. To make matters worse, Náhani had crawled in right behind him. Perspiration poured from his body as he struggled for oxygen, coughed, sneezed, and fought increasing claustrophobia. He was unable to bend either his knees or elbows. To add to the discomfort his hair had come untied.

Pulling himself into a cramped sitting position inside the whelping chamber, he handed the milk to the whimpering female. To his surprise, she gulped it down within seconds. Náhani squeezed in alongside her and sniffed the trap briefly. Not waiting for the dust to settle, Greg switched off the flashlight, managed to turn around, and re-entered the suffocating tunnel. At the bend he thought of taking the auxiliary route, but feared it might be even smaller. He could feel Náhani's hot breath on the soles of his feet as he pulled and pushed himself toward the circle of light and fresh air that seemed to be a mile away. Twenty-two wolves stood watching when he emerged from the tunnel.

Once outside, he and Náhani rushed to the lake for a five-minute swim. He suddenly became aware that the queen wolf was depending on him to do what she realized no wolf could do. He also had the feeling that she may have communicated this to the other wolves. At any rate, she appeared anxious for him to return to the den.

When he arrived, he was shaken to find that the little female had not emerged. If he could only persuade her to face away from him in one those narrow tunnels, he could grab the trap, depress the springs with both hands, and free her without fear that she would turn and attack him.

If he was unable to force her to leave the chamber, he would have to bring in enough two-inch-diameter poles to fence her off while he reached underneath and released the rusty trap.

The other wolves continued to watch from a distance. They seemed to realize what Greg was trying to do. He made two more excruciating trips into the underground chamber, taking a pan of water each time. As long as he imitated certain wolf sounds, the little female allowed him to touch her head and scratch her chin; but if he moved a hand toward the trap, she snarled and chomped. Náhani also warned him.

The trap was old and rusty. It must have been forgotten by the trapper two winters ago. To open it might require more strength than Greg could muster. Trappers acquired the necessary leverage to depress the springs by "breaking" the trap across a leg just behind the knee. There was no way of opening the jaws in the conventional manner inside that whelping chamber.

He suffered the same claustrophobia each time he squeezed through the long tunnel. On the third trip he foolishly decided to exit by way of the auxiliary passage. Halfway through he became entangled in a maze of ropelike tree roots. He was unable to fill his lungs with air. At the same time his leg muscles cramped. Finally he worked his hand to the sheath of his side knife by turning on one side. During the half hour it took to cut the obstructing roots away, Náhani lay at his feet and snored. Greg was too exhausted to enter the den again that day.

On the following morning a ruckus among the wolves awakened him. He rushed to the den. The little female sat at the entrance while nearly every male in the pack paced back and forth, growled, and sniffed the female's rear end. False oestrus, a condition sometimes brought on by the shock of a painful accident. Greg noticed that her trapped hind leg was badly swollen, a condition that probably eased some of the pain, but it also indicated that circulation below the pastern had been shut off. Gangrene would certainly follow, and within a matter of hours. When he approached with Náhani, the little wolf slunk back into the den.

Still dreading that narrow tunnel, and still emerging each time with his body covered with mud of his own sweat, Greg began to build a shield of short branch lengths to place between him and the wolf. She became more friendly with every visit until at last she did not snarl when he picked up the trap. But the presence of oestrual blood caused a constant tumult among the males. On every trip as Greg shoved the short poles ahead of him, he pushed aside one of several males occupying the tunnels. Their scrambling back and forth not only filled the passageways with dust and used up precious oxygen but also made the soft, sandy loam more hazardous.

Even before the shield between Greg and the female was finished, his flashlight batteries went dead. Total darkness as well as hot, heavy-breathing wolves in the tunnels now caused his claustrophobia to reach panic proportion. He probed under the shield for the trap. The springs were too rusty and too strong for his hands alone. When he tried to get his knee under the trap, the wolf shrieked with pain, knocked the shield apart, and rushed into the auxiliary tunnel where noisy fights ensued. Although he should have known what to expect when he went to crawl out by the shorter regular tunnel, he bumped squarely into Náhani. An inch at a time he was able to push her and persuade her to back out.

Finally, in the open air again, he saw the little female dragging the trap toward the beach, at the same time fighting off her own mate and other males. Although mated for life, a male wolf will try to mount any female canid in heat—even a female dog or coyote—unless the oestrual period occurs among all females at the same time in a pack situation or separately during pack breakup.

With large rocks, Greg blocked both entrances to the den then rushed to camp to get the nylon rope. The little female was rapidly communicating her distrust to the other wolves. Greg would have given up at this point, but Náhani, always at his side, seemed to bolster his hope. An hour later when the trapped wolf hobbled back to the den entrance and began to remove the blocking stones, Greg dropped a slip noose around the trap and threw the other end of the rope across an over-head spruce branch. Trusting Náhani to prevent an attack by the other wolves, he lifted the screaming female two feet above the ground by pulling the rope. He stepped quickly behind the tree, reached around with both arms in order to use the trunk for a fulcrum, grabbed the trap, compressed the springs, and freed the wolf in about seven seconds.

Greg ran immediately to the den entrances and cleared away the rocks, but the little female refused to enter. She ran in and out among the trees, shrieked, and slashed at every wolf within reach.

At last, exhausted, she seemed to calm. But there was neither delight nor relief in Náhani's expression. The panting little female moved from wolf to wolf, wagging her tail and whining. She was clearly out of her senses. Then she saw Greg with the roll of rope around one arm. Baring her teeth, she dropped her head and tail in the attack attitude and started slowly for the young Indian. He spoke softly to her as she advanced. Náhani stepped in front of him.

Ignoring the queen wolf's growl, the insane little female attempted to attack. With one mighty lunge, Náhani seized her throat and killed her.

While the other wolves looked on, the big silver-white stared into each face. Gradually the pack dispersed, some to the dens, some to the sunning shelf above timber line.

Greg picked up the lifeless body and the trap. Náhani followed. He buried the wolf in deep duff near the beach. Then he tied the trap to a low branch three feet above the runway where the other wolves would have to smell it whenever they left the denning complex. He wanted every wolf to remember and hate that instrument for all time.

CHAPTER FIFTEEN

To Be Allowed to Live

RICK BASS

RICK BASS *was born in 1958 and majored in petroleum geology at Utah State University. He worked in the oil industry in the southern United States before abandoning his scientific career to devote himself to writing. His short stories appear in collections such as* O. Henry Prize Stories *(1989) and* Best American Short Stories *(1992). His books have included* The Deer Pasture (1985), Wild to the Heart *(1988), and* Winter: Notes from Montana *(1991). As he writes in* The Ninemile Wolves *(1992), "May we all never be judged by anything so harshly or hold to as strict a life or unremitting of borders as the ones we try to place on and around wolves." Rick Bass lives on a ranch in northern Montana.*

THE DAY AFTER the old male was shot, the second pup died. It too starved up in the rock and ice country of Glacier National Park, just a few miles from the release site.

The remaining pup—the wild one still left at Marion—had disappeared. After nine days of looking for tracks and sign, and howling and listening, and checking the dozen traps they'd laid for it, no recent wolf activity could be detected.

The entire pack had been trapped in the political maze. Only the alpha female came out at the bottom, and she was heading south, along the far shores of Flathead Lake, passing right through the little town of

Bigfork, where dogs roam the streets in large numbers, though they all escaped with their lives that night. Her radio signals showed that she passed right next to the little hydro dam powerhouse in the downtown area. Flathead Lake—the largest freshwater lake in the West—barred her return to Marion.

There were touching reports of people seeing her here and there. She had to be lonely. Wolves are the most social mammals in this part of the world, except (maybe) for humans. One old woman in Rattlesnake Canyon just outside of Missoula, Irene Newman, said she spotted a wolf in her backyard orchard, just resting in the shade. Newman heard her five dogs barking and looked out her window and saw a wolf "sauntering up the draw behind the house."

Newman went outside and called to the wolf. "I see you," she told the wolf, and the wolf stopped, looked at Newman, and then stepped back behind an apple tree.

"You're not hiding, I can see you," Newman said, and the wolf peeked around the tree and looked up at her—just stood there, looking at her.

At the time, Dale Harms of the USF&WS [U.S. Fish and Wildlife Service] said that the black female's radio-collar signals showed she'd gone into the Rattlesnake area the day before, and he indicated to the press that this was the black female—the wolf that showed up behind Newman's apple tree. But Newman describes *her* wolf as being gray, despite the radio signals showing there was a black wolf in her orchard, not a gray one (according to Harms).

"She was big and gray with reddish tips on the end of her tail. And she had great big beautiful gray ears," Newman said.

The Marion female was as black as wet coal, from the nose to tail, except for her green eyes; there couldn't have been that big a mistake.

"I kept talking to her the whole time, and she kept looking at me and my dogs," Newman said. "Then she just moseyed along."

Once the alpha female was down near Missoula, the way for her to get back to Marion would be to turn back west, rather than continuing on south and east toward Yellowstone. West would also take her toward central Idaho, where many wolves have been reported, though never (except for one dead one) verified until 1992. This is what she did, moving back north and west, crossing over into the Ninemile Valley, and there the black alpha female found what biologists had not been able to: another wolf in Montana, outside of the national park, a lone wolf that had probably come over from Idaho. Was it Irene Newman's "she" wolf? Perhaps; if it was indeed yet another wolf, and not a big coyote. At any rate, the black female found this big gray male, and they mated.

No one knows for sure what drew the female to the big male in the Ninemile Valley. She could have heard his howls on the wind—researchers say that howls can be heard by humans at distances up to four, sometimes even five or six miles, and there's no real telling at what distance other wolves can hear each other, or at what distances they can pick up their own species' scent. The encouraging thing about the Ninemile male was that he just appeared. It makes me think that even if one wolf got down to Yellowstone, others would then find it. Wolves have a lovely way of coming out of the wood-work, when game populations are high and winters are mild.

One thing that's strange and wonderful about the species is the way they go for one extra-long trip before settling down to den in April. They often go farther on these road trips than they've ever been before. Biolo-gists who tell you on the one hand not to anthropo-morphize will turn right around and state flatly that the wolves know they're going to be cooped up with the pups and want to go for one last adventure.

The Ninemile née Marion female was no exception: On March 30th, 1990, a pilot picked up her signal and found her all the way over near Lolo Pass with—and this is more encouragement in a story that, at times, needs it—*two* other wolves.

The male and female finished their adventure, came back home to the Ninemile, dug the den near a field owned by two ranchers, Ralph and Bruce Thisted, and settled in to give birth. The third wolf wasn't seen again.

It was a small pack—just the two adults, and then in April, six pups (three gray and three black). The male hunted whitetail fawns and dragged them back to the den while the mother stayed with the pups. In a larger, more complex pack, there are often aunts and sometimes uncles who baby-sit for the mother so she can get out of the den, and other pack members will help bring down game. It's a dangerous business, hunting—wolves often sustain broken ribs and cracked skulls while dragging down adult ungulates. It's one of the hideous, lovely dances of nature, the way the young newborn ungulates are easy to catch—how in the spring, when predators need extra food for their young, the woods are alive with soft, easy prey. Of course it's sad. I've heard that in parts of Canada, moose have evolved so that all the mothers drop their calves within twenty-four to forty-eight hours of each other—every moose mother in the forest dropping her calf, like acorns falling during a high wind, so that *some* calf survival is ensured. The sheer logistics save, by luck and chance, 60 percent of the calves, because while the wolves are busy gorging on this windfall of baby moose, there's not enough time to go around and catch them all, and by that third day, the baby moose are good runners. The moose population's future (and therefore the wolves') is protected.

The wolf-pack members can rarely afford hunting-sustained injuries, especially when there are pups to feed. It's a fine system, as long as you're not one of the baby moose that get caught, or one of the spotted fawns. The fawns are easier to drag back to the den. Of course, any one of those male spotted fawns might have grown up to become antlered bucks, which then might have wandered across the cross hairs of some rich out-of-state hunter's rifle scope, thereby capitulating the various and related direct and indirect influx of moneys into the state's economy. But there are too many deer, record numbers of deer—neither the state nor the hunters should fear competition, nor should economics enter a matter of law ("but he murdered a *poor* man, Judge . . . "). There is a debt to be paid, and it is in the wolf's favor. We owe the wolf a huge payment for the misery we exacted in developing and taming the dry rangelands of the West into dusty factories of meat.

The other thing biologists—some biologists—tell you to watch out for, besides putting desired human traits on wolves, is symbolism. Joe Fontaine, another of the USF&WS biologists working the northern Rockies, warns, "Don't make the wolf bear your burden." Renée Askins, head of the Wolf Fund in Moose, Wyoming, praises the symbolism not of wolves, but of the wolf's return, and airs specifically her hopes for the return of the wolf to Yellowstone. Askins, who has a doctorate in biology from Yale, once raised captive pups in Michigan and has never been the same; that was twenty-one years ago.

"Reintroducing wolves to Yellowstone is an act of making room, of giving up the notion of 'bigger, better, and more,' to hold onto 'complete, balanced, and whole,'" Askins writes. "It is an act of giving back, a realigning, a recognition that we make ecological and ethical mistakes and learn from them, and what we learn can inform our actions. Thus reintroducing wolves to Yellowstone is a symbolic act just as exterminating wolves from the West was a symbolic act," says Askins.

■

But we have drifted off the scent. Wolves eat fawns in the spring and early summer. There are too many deer in the Ninemile Valley—way too many. In the absence of natural predators, it may be argued, *any* deer are too many. By selecting so heavy-handedly for deer and against predators, we have disrupted the amplitudes of the natural rise-and-fall cycles of both predators and prey, so that now we see only the rise-rise-rise cycle.

Things were working real nice in the Ninemile Valley for the mother and father wolf and the six pups. None of that Marion trauma. Sometimes the cows would watch the mother and her pups play at the edge of the cows' meadow.

What you may think is coming did not come. The wolves did not bother the cows.

Sometimes, when the mother and father wolf—the alphas—and their pack head off on their end-of-March, first-of-April "last flings," the females don't make it back to the den in time to give birth. John Murray, a writer in Alaska, tells about one alpha female in Denali National Park who was trotting home from one such trip and who had to stop and give birth out in the middle of the tundra—had to lie down in just a small depression out of the wind. It was twenty-four hours before she could move the pups to her real den, so in the meantime the rest of the pack brought her snowshoe hares and stood guard to protect her and the pups from any wandering-by grizzlies. It's a lovely story, and so close to our own species' Christmas story that I feel a most unscientific empathy . . .

June 10th, 1990, was the last time anyone saw the Ninemile female alive. One of the Thisted brothers—

the two old ranchers who observed the wolves at length—saw the mother sitting at the edge of their meadow with the pups swarming her, licking her.

On July 4th, a fisherman found her collar floating in the Ninemile River. It had been cut and thrown from the bridge. By all indications, the rarest of things had been killed: A "good" wolf that would have nothing to do with cows. She had probably had nothing to do with the killings up in Marion—that had been almost certainly the coyotes, or the old tooth-worn male, who had had to do the hunting for her while she stayed in the den with those first ill-fated pups. She would have been a good mother, would have been a fine example to her new pups about how not to bring down cows, and we miss her. I miss her.

The principal business in the Ninemile Valley is wintering cattle and providing spring birthing grounds before turning the cows out onto the surrounding federal lands for summer grazing. It's been that way for a long time. It's just like almost every small valley in Montana. The big gray male, the loner, was left to raise the pups by himself. I remember reading about it in the newspaper almost every day that summer. The sadness of the female's absence lingered. She was gone, but hard to forget.

CHAPTER SIXTEEN

On the Raising of Wolves and a New Ethology

BARRY LOPEZ

*BARRY LOPEZ was born in Port Chester, New York,
in 1945. He grew up in New York and southern
California and has become perhaps the foremost natural
history essayist in America. He is a contributing editor to*
Harper's *and* North American Review *and is on the
editorial advisory board of* Orion Nature Quarterly. *His
books include* Winter Count *(1982),* Arctic Dreams
(1986), and Crossing Open Ground *(1988). He is
the recipient of the American Book Award, the John
Burroughs Medal, and the Award in Literature from the
American Academy and Institute of Arts & Letters.
He currently lives in western Oregon.*

I AM NOT AN AUTHORITY on wolves. I do not think
my experiences are universal, and I do not wish to en-
courage other people to raise wolves. Wolves don't be-
long living with people. It's as simple as that. Having
done it once, naïvely, I would never do it again. Most
people I know who have raised wolves feel the same
way. All too often the wolf's life ends tragically and
its potential for growth while it lives is smothered. I
am grateful for the knowledge I have gained but if
I'd known what it would cost I don't think I would
have asked.

■

Prairie and River came to us from a wildlife park
through the intervention of a friend and were three

weeks old when they arrived. We bottle-fed them and, as is usually the case with young wolves, or dogs, they were intensely interested in everything around them. Canines use their mouths, I think, in much the same way we use our hands, especially when they are young. They are not trying to eat everything they encounter, they are simply trying to get a feeling for whatever it is. And the wolves felt everything. By the time they were six weeks old we had anything we valued stored three feet off the floor.

In these first few weeks, Prairie and River howled mournfully, perhaps sensing their parents' distance or their isolation from others like themselves. They ate ravenously and seemed always to be at one of two extremes: sleeping, sprawled like beanbags in the middle of the floor, or tearing through the house in pursuit of each other or imaginary beings. When they were seven weeks old they had a single, short, bloody fight during which the female, Prairie, got the best of the male, River. We never saw another fight as serious, though which animal usually deferred to the other afterward changed several times.

They never tried to harm us when they were puppies (or later), though they jerked at our hair hard enough almost to wrench it from our skulls, and they would scratch us inadvertently with their claws and sharp milk teeth. And though we were not afraid of them when they got larger, they occasionally tried the imaginations of our friends with their antics. One day a woman left her infant son on a blanket on our living-room floor and turned her back to talk with us. Behind her were the wolves, whose hiding place was under the wood stove. The pups came out into the open (overcoming their fear of a strange adult), anxious to get a closer look at the baby, a living creature (I was thinking they were thinking) close to their own size and, more importantly, one who also lived in that twelve-inch-high zone next to the floor where they lived.

With great hesitancy, ready to flee at the first sign of discovery, jabbing the air nervously, high and low, for some clue to the creature, they finally got up to the edge of the baby's blanket. Anxious to draw the baby into their world but still afraid of the adult whose back was turned only inches away, they took an obvious but frightening step—they took hold of the baby's blanket and began pulling him away. At that moment the mother turned around and the surprised wolves—scrambling frantically for traction on the hardwood floor—bolted for their hideout under the wood stove.

Another time, when they were about a year old, Prairie and River "attacked" Sandy, my wife. We had had friends to dinner and we wanted them to see the wolves before they left. It was very late, so we took a flashlight and led them out through the woods. The wolves had been asleep but they jumped up as we drew near. We were at the fence for only a few minutes, sweeping the flashlight around their pen, before we said good night to our friends and they departed.

I felt guilty about waking the wolves up, about invading their privacy. I wouldn't wake a child up for friends to see in the middle of the night. Sandy and I exchanged some thoughts about this and she went back to the pen without the flashlight. I went into the house. As she entered the pen the wolves immediately began to push her around, slamming against her with their bodies and soft-biting her arms and legs. They were fast enough and strong enough, of course, to have hurt her seriously, but they didn't. Our intuitive feeling was that they were angry. Other people who have worked with wolves in enclosures have had similar experiences. It is almost as if the animals were warning you of the limits of friendship. What makes the message so strong, of course, is that it's coming from an animal that can kill you.

Although I am familiar with wild country, I learned, I think, several remarkable things simply by walking in the woods with River and Prairie and paying attention to what they did. We took them out on leashes. They often sought out ridges, high on the slopes of the mountain valley where we lived. I assumed at first that it was for the view but later it seemed it was for another reason as well. Here the air currents that moved strongly upslope in the afternoon reached them intact, not broken up, with the olfactory information they carried scattered, as happened when the winds blew through the trees.

The wolves moved deftly and silently in the woods and in trying to imitate them I came to walk more quietly and to freeze at the sign of slight movement. At first this imitation gave me no advantage, but after several weeks I realized I was becoming far more attuned to the environment we moved through. I heard more, for one thing, and, my senses now constantly alert, I occasionally saw a deer mouse or a grouse before they did. I also learned the several thousand acres we walked in well enough to find my way around in the dark. I never moved as quietly, or with the grace that they did, not with my upright stance and long limbs that caused my body to become entangled, and the ninety-degree angle at my ankle that caused my feet to catch. But I took from them the confidence to believe I could attune myself better to the woods by behaving as they did— minutely inspecting certain things, seeking vantage points, always sniffing at the air. I did, and felt vigorous, charged with alertness.

They moved always, it seemed one day, in search of clues.

◾

After these experiences, when I came in contact with Eskimo perceptions of the wolf I was much quicker to understand that the Eskimo "sees" differently from the way I see, and that I would likely never see as well in the wild as the Eskimo did, any more than I would ever see as well in the woods one day as Prairie and River.

◾

There were moments of pain and embarrassment with the wolves, times when we sensed how awful the pen must have been for them, as large as it was. The smoke from a slash fire at a logging site would drift through. They would sense fire but have nowhere to run. Deer would appear, and the wolves would race excitedly up and down, looking for a way out. A loose board would make a banging noise in a storm and terrify them. There were other incidents, though, ones that could almost make up for these. To see them leaping for falling leaves in October. To sleep with them in the pen at night and feel them drifting by, just brushing your fingertips with their fur.

I would often sit out in the woods next to the pen on sunny afternoons, reading and making notes. I enjoyed being around them.

One summer day, when the wolves were a little more than two years old, someone let them out. We never found out who. I think it must have been someone who believed all wild animals should be free but who did not know that wild animals raised in captivity are no longer wild. River was shot and killed by a man who told us later he wasn't sure what kind of animals they were but they looked wild and were trying to play with his neighbor's dogs, so he thought they might be rabid. With River lying there dead, Prairie bolted for the deep woods. The next day, when we got home (we were away at a funeral), she responded to Sandy's howling and came to her, lay down at her feet, trembling and disoriented.

Prairie's depression and disorientation lasted for weeks, long enough for us to consider putting her to sleep. Finally, with the aid of a young dog who befriended and supported her, she came around.

We buried River. While I was digging the grave I thought of all the wolves I had met and how many of those were dead. Killed by other wolves in pens that did not let an ostracized animal escape. Killed in scientific experiments. Poisoned by people who hated wolves. Shot by neighbors who feared them. Wolf pups that had been killed by animal caretakers because there were simply too many to be fed and housed, and no one had taken the responsibility to isolate the sexes when the females were in estrus. Killed by people who professed a love for wolves but who, because the wolf puppies wouldn't housebreak like dogs, or because they didn't look royal blooded enough after losing an ear or the tip of a tail in a fight, didn't want them around.

I didn't know what to say to the man who killed River. I didn't know what to say to River. I just stood there in an afternoon rain trying to remember what I'd learned in his presence.

■

I think, as the twentieth century comes to a close, that we are coming to an understanding of animals different from the one that has guided us for the past three hundred years. We have begun to see again, as our primitive ancestors did, that animals are neither imperfect imitations of men nor machines that can be described entirely in terms of endocrine secretions and neural impulses. Like us, they are genetically variable, and both the species and the individual are capable of unprecedented behavior. They are like us in the sense that we can figuratively talk of them as beings some of whose forms, movements, activities, and social organizations are analogous, but they are no more literally like us than are trees. To paraphrase Henry Beston, they move in another universe, as complete as we are, both of us caught at a moment in mid-evolution.

I do not think it possible to define completely the sort of animals men require in order to live. They are always changing and are different for different peoples. Nor do I think it possible that science can by itself produce the animal entire. The range of the human mind, the scale and depth of the metaphors the mind is capable of manufacturing as it grapples with the universe, stand in stunning contrast to the belief that there is only one reality, which is man's, or worse, that only one culture among the many on earth possesses the truth.

To allow mystery, which is to say to yourself, "There could be more, there could be things we don't understand," is not to damn knowledge. It is to take a wider view. It is to permit yourself an extraordinary freedom: someone else does not have to be wrong in order that you may be right.

In the Western world, in the biological sciences, we have an extraordinary tool for discovery of knowledge about animals, together with a system for its classification; and through the existence of journals and libraries we have a system for its dissemination. But if we are going to learn more about animals—real knowledge, not more facts—we are going to have to get out into the woods. We are going to have to pay more attention to free-ranging as opposed to penned animals, which will require an unfamiliar patience. And we are going to have to find ways in which single, startling incidents in animal behavior, now discarded in the winnowing process of science's data assembly, can be preserved, can somehow be incorporated. And we are going to have to find a way, not necessarily to esteem, but at least not to despise intuition in the scientific process, for it is, as Kepler and Darwin and Einstein have said, the key.

The English philosopher Alfred North Whitehead, writing about human inquiry into the nature of the universe, said that in simply discussing the issues, the merest hint of dogmatic certainty is an exhibition of folly. This tolerance for mystery invigorates the imagination; and it is the imagination that gives shape to the universe.

The appreciation of the separate realities enjoyed by other organisms is not only no threat to our own reality, but the root of a fundamental joy. I learned from River that I was a human being and that he was a wolf and that we were different. I valued him as a creature, but he did not have to be what I imagined he was. It is with this freedom from dogma, I think, that the meaning of the words "the celebration of life" becomes clear.

CHAPTER SEVENTEEN
Wolf Kin & Humankind
MICHAEL W. FOX

MICHAEL W. FOX was born in 1937. He is an acclaimed animal behaviorist and serves as vice-president of the Humane Society of the United States. His numerous books on human–animal relationships include Inhumane Society *(1990). As he poignantly notes, " 'See me for what I am, not as you wish to use me' is the silent cry of the wilderness, of wolf, whale, forest, and ocean alike."*
He lives in Washington, D.C.

WOLVES, LIKE AMERICAN INDIANS, lived at peace with nature for thousands of years. Both were hunters, but neither would overkill or hunt for sport. Biologically, and for the Indian also spiritually, these hunters were an integral part of the ecosystem. Prey, such as deer, caribou, and moose, produce excess young, an evolutionary adaptation to anticipated disease and predation. Wolves regulate their numbers, killing off the sick and inferior, and so maintain herd quality and prevent overpopulation and ultimate overgrazing and death from starvation.

To preserve the wolf in captivity because he is such an intelligent and social animal—perhaps the most highly evolved land mammal in North America—is not enough. The ecosystem of which the wolf is an integral part must also be conserved wherever and whenever possible.

Wolves and Indians were exterminated when they ate the settler's livestock; but there was nothing else to eat since their natural prey had been eradicated to make room for the domestic stock. Indians were given reservations and the interests of white settlers were protected. Wolves need sanctuary and protection from trophy and fur hunters and trappers. In some wolf-free wildlife areas, surplus deer are killed off each year by wildlife management personnel; wolves could be put back in such places in order to restore the ecosystem. They are certainly more appropriate "managers" of deer and have a greater right to hunt than has modern man.

Once, all men supported themselves by hunting, but since modern man has domesticated livestock, hunting is no longer a necessity. It is a sport, a luxury, a service where excess deer must be culled, a crime when predators like wolves and cougars that have never killed farm stock and live miles from human habitation are killed for sport or fur. A crime against nature, because removing such predators upsets the ecological equilibrium and can destroy the ecosystem

In 1856, the chief of the Duwamish Indians foresaw the white man's demise—"He sees and claims the world for himself and fails to see that he is an integral part of the world."

When modern man can perceive that this is in fact true, he may be able to save the ecosystem of which he is a part but which today he is destroying and making into an impersonal global ecosystem. Man is linked with wolf and with all of nature. To break this link is to destroy the spirit of the earth and the essence of humanity within it.

Man, Evolution and Responsibility

Part of the creative genius of *Homo sapiens* is to see the things around him and convert them for his own uses and use them to satisfy his many needs. A rock may be shaped into a flint; a deer is potential food and clothing and fishing lines from skin and sinews; a tree, timber for a house; a river, a source of hydroelectric energy; a wilderness of shale, energy for our cities. As man evolves and explores the world around him, he discovers more that can satisfy and support society and the cancerlike, energy-consuming creations of technology.

The world is seen in terms of one's needs, and a new discovery, a new source of energy, or a faster or more productive machine is a mark of progress. The male ego is fed by values supporting growth, progress, and exploration and operates by controlling, manipulating and exploiting.

The tragic flaw in human perception, though, is that modern man does not really see the world as it really is. It is seen only in terms of how it can satisfy certain needs. "See me for what I am, not as you wish to use me," is the silent cry of wilderness, of wolf, whale, forest, and ocean alike.

Seeing an eagle, a puma, a wolf, or a whale as the thing in itself, no man could kill it without first questioning his own reasons for doing so. In seeing, such a man has matured at last beyond the primitive ego that feels pride and status in hunting and killing. He has matured by establishing a new connection in his brain and by breaking an old one that he inherited from his forefathers. The new connection gives him a greater awareness, which is the key to understanding life for what it is and others for what they are. The old connection tied him to the world, where the world of nature is merely an extension of himself, an egosphere, if you wish. Once broken, he becomes a free man, no longer controlled by or imposing his needs, values, and rights on others, be they wolves or other men. Other people, wolves, and indeed all living things suddenly have rights and intrinsic values in themselves. Their needs can now be seen and understood at last, and are no longer felt as a means or an obstacle to the fulfillment of one's own needs.

Yes, it is the overriding motive of conquest, which is the stamp of modern man as it was of our primitive hunter ancestors. For similar selfish reasons, man will strive to conquer cougar, wolf, deer, women, oceans, mountains, new continents, and even outer space. So preoccupied with such outer diversion, we have hardly begun to explore our "inner space"—the greatest conquest for man is the inner space of his being.

Once a man can see a tree, a wolf, or his fellow and value the other for what it, he, or she is, then his world will be very different. He will rediscover the brotherhood of humanity and reverence for all life, and foster this in others and in his children. Kinship with nature is the key to this awareness. No man can look inward, however, when he is looking at the world through the sights on his gun, which is a world view as narrow and destructive as his egocentric perception and values.

Man, a product of the creative/evolutionary process, now has the potential of this process in his consciousness and actions. He is a product of creation as he is creator himself. Being so, he is both animal and god: having a biological kinship with all life and a responsibility where his own actions or inactions, values and needs, can assist or destroy the evolutionary process. Mankind's destiny and the future of the world is our burden of responsibility and our price for the freedom to be.

CHAPTER EIGHTEEN

Conclusion: The Future of the Wolf

ROBERT H. BUSCH

*"The greatest danger to Timber Wolves lies in the future—
in the latter part of this century—when large areas of
big game range are no longer accessible . . . what will
be our attitude then? Will we be willing to share
deer, moose, caribou with the wolves?"*
DOUGLAS PIMLOTT (1961)

IT HAS BEEN three decades since these words were written, and in many ways, we are no closer today to conclusively answering these questions than we were thirty years ago.

However, the general attitude toward the wolf and other large predators has improved dramatically, and the horrible carnage imposed by humans on wolf populations is largely a thing of the past.

Today the wolf is absent from 95 percent of its former range in the lower United States. The largest remaining population is in northern Minnesota, where perhaps 1,700 wolves remain. Michigan and Wisconsin together harbor about 60 wolves, and Montana, Washington, and Idaho also conceal a combined population of about 60 wolves. Alaska has the highest U.S. wolf population, with about 7,000 wolves. Canada has a large and healthy wolf population of about 50,000. The largest wolf densities there are found in the Northwest Territories, the Yukon, and northern Ontario.

Although the wolf has been intensely studied over

the past three decades, much remains to be learned. At the Second North American Symposium on Wolves, held in Edmonton, Alberta, in August 1992, some of the topics listed as requiring further research included wolf genetics, disease, inbreeding, scent marking, dispersal factors, and wolf–prey interrelationships.

This last topic is of prime interest to biologists and conservationists. It is as a predator that the wolf has suffered the most in the past three decades, the victim of wolf management programs by various governments across the continent.

It is generally accepted that wolf predation can be a limiting factor for prey populations, but it is very difficult to measure the magnitude of this factor when compared to others such as overhunting and loss of habitat. The past thirty years have seen much debate on this issue, and as Dr. David Mech says, "I am not sure we'll ever answer all the questions relating to the effects of wolf predation to completely satisfy everybody."

■

One of the most poorly conceived wolf management programs took place in British Columbia in the early 1980s. In 1983, the British Columbia government announced plans to kill 80 percent of the wolves in the northeastern Peace and Omineca districts in order "to support moose and deer populations."

Conservationists have long argued that such support is often biologically unsound, and in fact serves only to appease the strong hunting lobby. It is somewhat ironic that many of the fish and game departments across North America do, in fact, exist primarily to support the hunting and fishing interests that finance the departments' very existence through the sale of hunting and fishing licenses. And one of the key philosophical questions today is whether "sport" hunters have a greater right to kill deer or moose than do wolves, which kill in order to survive.

Perhaps the best comment on the political management of wildlife was penned by biologist Mark Stalmaster, who once wrote that "Wildlife management decisions should be based on sound scientific knowledge, not on the desires of special interest groups, public outcry, or inane governmental directives." And additional long-term scientific knowledge concerning the wolf is direly needed. Many declines in ungulate (deer and moose) populations blamed on wolves may in fact be the result of natural lows in population cycles. The long-term wolf study on Michigan's Isle Royale, initiated in the 1950s, may prove to be invaluable in this regard.

In the case of the British Columbia wolf management plan, hunting associations supplied much of the financing for the wolf kill. To supply additional funding, the British Columbia government announced a plan for a lottery, first prize being a hunting trip to Zimbabwe, further underlining the close ties between the government wolf kill and the prohunting lobby. Despite a government report that moose and deer numbers had declined due to loss of habitat, overhunting, and a series of severe winters, the wolf once again had been chosen as a convenient scapegoat. The Wildlife Society of Canada and the Wildlife Biologists section of the Canadian Society of Biologists reviewed the technical data behind the program and stated that "There is no biological basis or biological justification for the wolf control program currently being conducted in northeast British Columbia." The public outcry was strong, but over 400 wolves died before the program was abandoned.

A similar debacle ensued when the Alaskan government announced its plans in 1992 to kill 300–400 wolves in the 1993 management season. In the decade since the British Columbia wolf kill, a number of conservation groups have emerged as well-organized and well-financed lobbies for the rights of animals. As soon as the Alaskan plan was announced, groups such as the Wolf Fund and Friends of Animals were quick to denounce the proposal. Animal rights activists and concerned environmentalists alike united in an Alaskan travel boycott, and announced plans to boycott Alaska-made products. Despite Alaskan Governor Walter Hickel's bizarre pronouncement that "You can't let nature just run wild," in the face of massive public pressure the program was quietly canceled. Six months later, the plan was revised to allow the killing of wolves as long as the hunters are 90 meters from their aircraft. Conservationists quickly announced that they would revive their threat of an Alaska travel boycott. As Dr. Lu Carbyn, a biologist with the Canadian Wildlife Service, has stated, government wolf control "has become socially unacceptable."

In Alaska, aerial shooting of wolves was outlawed in

the 1970s, but it has been replaced by aerial harassment of wolves, followed by the land-and-kill technique. In the fall of 1992, a polling company found that 74 percent of Alaskans polled were opposed to aerial wolf killings. And U.S. Fish and Wildlife agent Dave Purinton estimates that 99.9 percent of the land-and-kill shootings are illegal. It can only be hoped that the same public pressure that has been so successful in halting government wolf kills can also be focused on irresponsible wolf hunting practices.

Another area in which the swelling tide of public opinion has had a positive effect on the wolf is that of the dictates of fashion. The shift in attitude against the wearing of animal furs has reduced the trapping pressure on the wolf and other furbearers. A typical gray wolf pelt that sold for $800 in the mid-1980s now brings just $75, and many trappers no longer actively pursue the wolf.

Replacing the trapping threat is the increasing expansion of farms and ranches into wolf country. Since the wolf is an opportunistic hunter, it is inevitable that wolf predation on livestock will occur when farms spread into wolf territory.

All too often, though, the extent of such predation is overestimated by anxious farmers and ranchers. In northern Minnesota, despite a wolf population of over 1,700 wolves, less than 1 percent of ranches are affected by wolf predation. About 25 "problem" wolves are killed annually by government agents, but sadly an additional 200 wolves are killed by poachers and wolf haters. The same 1 percent figure crops up again in a Canadian study: only 1 percent of 1,608 wolf scats collected in Manitoba's Riding Mountain National Park contained any traces of livestock remains. But despite the very low incidence of wolf predation on livestock, many governments have been quick to provide sweeping wolf-killing powers to farmers and ranchers.

For example, in Alberta, landowners, or those with permission of landowners, are allowed to kill any number of wolves at any time of the year without a license, as long as the wolves are killed on private property, leased grazing lands, or within five miles of such lands. Many conservationists have recommended the suspension of this generous policy, especially in southwest Alberta in order to enhance the recovery of the Montana wolf population. A 1987 U.S. Fish and Wildlife study stated that the recovery of wolves in Montana would certainly depend in part on the survival of southern Alberta wolves and their migration into Montana.

As humans continue to expand into wilderness areas, livestock predation by wolves and other predators is unavoidable. Passive measures such as the use of livestock guard dogs or electric fences have largely proved either ineffective or too expensive. Financial compensation for livestock losses is part of the answer, but there is also a need for public education on the proper disposal of animal carcasses and other attractions to predators. In one U.S. Fish and Wildlife study, 63 percent of 111 Minnesota farmers surveyed merely left their dead livestock in place, or just dragged the carcasses to the edge of the woods. It is a tribute to the wary nature of the wolf that lifestock predation is not higher under such attractive conditions.

■

Perhaps the most controversial wolf issue today is that of wolf reintroduction programs. In many areas, the lack of predators has resulted in an overpopulation of ungulates. In parts of Yellowstone National Park, for example, elk, deer, moose, and bison have overgrazed vast swaths of park. Many ecologists believe that several packs of wolves could survive as predators within the park, filling an ecological niche that now remains empty.

In the United States, the U.S. Fish and Wildlife Service is the chief agency responsible for reintroduction programs, in conjunction with state wildlife agencies and several private conservation groups. The original Northern Rocky Mountain Wolf Recovery Plan was developed in 1980, and revised in 1987. The plan has identified three areas for potential wolf reintroduction in the western United States: the Northwest Montana area, the central Idaho wilderness area, and the Greater Yellowstone area. It recommends natural recolonization of wolves in the Montana and Idaho areas, and suggests reintroduction to the Yellowstone area. The goal in each area is a minimum of ten breeding pairs for a minimum of three successive years. This equates to a resident population of about 100 wolves in each area.

In 1985, 60 percent of Yellowstone visitors polled agreed that "If wolves can't return to Yellowstone on their own, then we should put them back ourselves." But the plan is not without its opponents. One angry individual wrote that "the wolf was destroyed because it was undesirable to human well-being." And Montana Senator Conrad Burns wildly predicted that if wolves were returned to Yellowstone, "there'll be a dead child within a year." (Despite common folklore to the contrary, there is no documented record of any human fatality due to wolves anywhere in North America.)

Wolves may well return naturally to the Yellowstone wilderness before the official reintroduction program gets underway. In 1992, a lone male was shot by a moose hunter near the southern boundary of Yellowstone National Park.

Wolves that return naturally to Yellowstone would probably migrate from northern Montana's Glacier National Park area, where a small, healthy wolf population survives. Wolf recovery is occurring naturally in Montana, and the state now boasts a total population of about 50 wolves. The U.S. Fish and Wildlife Service may bolster this population with wolves imported from Canada. In one 1990 poll, two-thirds of Montana residents polled were in favor of reintroducing wolves to the Glacier Park wilderness area.

The loudest opposition to the plan has come from members of the ranching community, who fear massive losses to reintroduced predators. One such resident complained that "they'll want to reintroduce the sabretooth tiger next." Various conservation groups and government bodies have attempted to reassure these individuals through promises of financial compensation for livestock predation. Defenders of Wildlife, a large conservation group, has a standing offer to pay for such losses. The compensation has averaged about $1,700 per year since 1987. Another solution may be the zone system of wildlife management. According to this system, zones of virgin land are allocated primarily for wildlife, a buffer zone is set up along their perimeters, and then inner zones are established where wolves can exist only if they do not negatively affect humans. Problem wolves in the innermost zone are relocated or destroyed.

In Idaho, there may be up to 15 wolves currently living in the central Idaho wilderness area. A 1992 poll showed that 72 percent of Idahoans surveyed were in favor of having wolves in the wilderness and roadless areas of central Idaho.

As Steven H. Fritts, the Northern Rocky Mountain Wolf Coordinator for the U.S. Fish and Wildlife Service, has succinctly written, "The key to wolf population recovery in the northwestern United States lies in human tolerance—a relatively new perspective in our society."

■

There is no question that if wolves are to survive, sufficient protected habitat must exist for both the wolf and its prey. In Canada, only 1.2 percent of the wolf's range is protected as parks or preserves. And in many of Canada's parks, hunters are allowed to shoot wolves during prescribed seasons. The World Wildlife Fund (Canada) has recommended that no hunting be allowed within park boundaries and that buffer zones be established outside the boundaries to ease the problem of hunters "accidentally" straying within park boundaries. The U.S. situation is less promising. In the United States, very few areas still remain outside the proposed recovery areas that could sustain a healthy wolf population.

As is the case for any beleaguered species, it is crucial that the myths surrounding the wolf be dispelled through public education. U.S. Fish and Wildlife Service studies have shown that people with fuller knowledge about wolves tend to have more positive attitudes toward them. In many parks, wolf appreciation programs help to educate the public about the place of predators in the ecosystem and to eliminate the "good animal/bad animal" labels so often applied to wild creatures. One such education technique is the use of wolf howl programs. In central Ontario, a wolf howl program in Algonquin Provincial Park has proved to be a resounding success in promoting positive interactions with wolves. From 1963 to 1980, over 38,000 people attended public wolf howls. Over half of those who raised their own human voices to the sky were successful in eliciting a response from the park's wild wolf population.

With increased public education, additional scientific research, and improved management practices, the future of the wolf does indeed seem more positive than the picture painted even a decade ago. When one also considers the wolf's high reproductive rate and natural intelligence, it seems certain that future generations will continue to be thrilled by the quivering cry of wild wolf songs.

■

In 1973, the Wolf Manifesto of the International Union for the Conservation of Nature declared that "wolves have a right to exist in a wild state . . . in no way related to their known value to mankind." It is my fervent hope that today's society has finally learned to accept such rights for all wild creatures, and that a society has evolved that has learned to accept the other animals with which we share this planet.

For despite the lofty pedestal upon which we place ourselves, man is merely one of the millions of species that inhabit planet Earth. Man, according to Plato, is just a "biped without feathers," or as modern sage Stephen W. Hawking describes us, "an advanced breed of monkeys on a minor planet of a very average star." And it is at the option of man, the supreme predator, that the survival of the wolf and all other fellow animals will ultimately depend.

FOR FURTHER READING

For a global overview of wolves, see *Wolves of the World,* by F. H. Harrington and P. C. Pacquet (Park Ridge, NJ: Noyes Publications, 1982).

The Wolves of North America, by Stanley Young (Washington, DC: American Wildlife Institute, 1944), is the best early summary of information on North American wolves. It also contains an excellent bibliography. *The World of the Wolf,* by R. J. Rutter and Douglas Pimlott (Philadelphia: Lippincott, 1968) provides a more recent summary. The best current summary is contained in *Trail of the Wolf,* by R. D. Lawrence (Toronto: Key Porter Books, 1993).

For a historical review of the wolf in North America, see *The Wolf in North American History,* by Stanley Young (Caldwell, ID: Caxton Printers, 1946) or Roderick Nash's *Wilderness and the American Mind* (New Haven, CT: Yale University Press, 1967).

Barry Lopez's *Of Wolves and Men* (New York: Scribner's, 1978) gives an exhaustive history of the changing attitudes towards the wolf.

David Mech's *The Wolf: The Ecology and Behavior of an Endangered Species* (Minneapolis: University of Minnesota Press, 1981) provides an excellent technical summary of wolf ecology. *The Wolves of Isle Royale,* Fauna of the National Parks of the United States Series 7 (Washington, DC: U.S. Department of the Interior, 1966), by the same author, is one of the first serious field studies of the wolf. For further ecological data, see *Ecological Studies of the Timber Wolf in Northeastern Minnesota,* by D. Mech and L. D. Frenzel, Forest Research Paper NC-52 (St. Paul, MN: U.S. Department of Agriculture, North Central Forest Experiment Station, 1971), D. L. Allen's *The Wolves of Minong: Their Vital Role in a Wild Community* (Boston: Houghton Mifflin, 1979), or *Wolf Ecology and Prey Relationships on Isle Royale,* by R. O. Peterson, National Park Service Scientific Monograph Series No. 11 (Washington, DC: National Park Service, 1977).

The Soul of the Wolf (New York: Lyons & Burford, 1980), by Michael W. Fox, details insights into the complex interrelationships between humans and wolves.

Monte Hummel and Sherry Pettigrew's *Wild Hunters* (Toronto: Key Porter Books, 1991) summarizes the many threats currently facing wolves and other predators in North America.

WOLF CONSERVATION ORGANIZATIONS

Alaska Wildlife Alliance, P.O. Box 6953, Anchorage, AL 99502

Friends of the Wolf, P.O. Box 21032, Glebe Postal Outlet, Ottawa, Canada K1S 2HO

International Wolf Center, 1396 Hwy 169, Ely, MN 55731

North American Wolf Foundation, Inc., Rt. 133-98 Essex Road, Ipswich, MA 01938

Northern Michigan Wolf Sanctuary, 117 Case Street, Negaunee, MI 49866

The Wolf Fund, P.O. Box 471, Moose, WY 83012

Wild Canid Survival & Research Center, P.O. Box 760, Eureka, MO 63025

Wolf Haven, 3111 Offut Lake Road, Tenino, WA 98589

Wolf Park, Battle Ground, IN 47920

WOLF NEWSLETTER

Wolf Newsletter, P.O. Box 29, Lafayette, IN 47902-0029

PERMISSIONS

"Thinking Like a Mountain" is excerpted from *A Sand County Almanac, with other essays on conservation from Round River* by Aldo Leopold. Copyright © 1949, 1953, 1966, renewed 1977, 1981 by Oxford University Press, Inc. Reprinted by permission of Oxford University Press, Inc.

"Growing Up Wild" is excerpted from *Secret Go the Wolves* by R. D. Lawrence. Copyright © 1980 by R. D. Lawrence. Reprinted by permission of Henry Holt and Company, Inc.

"Good Old Uncle Albert" is excerpted from *Never Cry Wolf* by Farley Mowat (Toronto: McClelland and Stewart Limited). Copyright © 1963, 1973, 1993 by Farley Mowat. Reprinted by permission of Farley Mowat.

"The East Fork Wolves" is excerpted from *The Wolves of Mount McKinley* by Adolph Murie (Washington: U.S. Government Printing Office, 1944, and Seattle: University of Washington Press, 1985). Reprinted by permission of University of Washington Press.

"Arctic Fall" is excerpted from Chapter 12 of *Arctic Wild* by Lois Crisler. Copyright © 1958 by Lois Crisler. Reprinted by permission of HarperCollins Publishers, Inc.

"At Home with the Arctic Wolf" is excerpted from *The Arctic Wolf: Living With the Pack*. Copyright © 1988 by L. David Mech, reprinted with permission of the publisher, Voyageur Press, Inc., 123 North Second Street, Stillwater, MN 55082, U.S.A., 1-800-888-9653.

"Adaptation" is excerpted from *White Wolf: Living With an Arctic Legend* by Jim Brandenburg. Copyright © 1988 by the author, reprinted by permission of NorthWord Press, Inc.